中华人民共和国地理标志
GI
GEOGRAPHICAL INDICATION OF P.R.CHINA

《中华人民共和国政府与欧洲联盟地理标志保护与合作协定》

中欧地理标志产品互认互保名录

（中国产品第一批）

汉英对照

国家知识产权局 组织编写

知识产权出版社
全国百佳图书出版单位
—北京—

图书在版编目（CIP）数据

《中华人民共和国政府与欧洲联盟地理标志保护与合作协定》中欧地理标志产品互认互保名录：中国产品．第一批：汉英对照／国家知识产权局组织编写．—北京：知识产权出版社，2022.4

ISBN 978-7-5130-7757-6

Ⅰ．①中…　Ⅱ．①国…　Ⅲ．①地理—标志—产品标识—中国—名录—汉、英　Ⅳ．①F760.5-62

中国版本图书馆 CIP 数据核字（2021）第 204415 号

责任编辑：王小玲　　责任校对：王　岩
封面设计：智兴设计室·张国仓　　责任印制：刘译文
文字编辑：刘林波

《中华人民共和国政府与欧洲联盟地理标志保护与合作协定》中欧地理标志产品互认互保名录
——中国产品第一批（汉英对照）
国家知识产权局　组织编写

出版发行：知识产权出版社有限责任公司	网　址：http:// www.ipph.cn
社　址：北京市海淀区气象路 50 号院	邮　编：100081
责编电话：010-82000860 转 8252	责编邮箱：shdwxl2010@163.com
发行电话：010-82000860 转 8101/8102	发行传真：010-82000893/82005070/82000270
印　刷：天津嘉恒印务有限公司	经　销：新华书店、各大网上书店及相关专业书店
开　本：880mm×1230mm　1/16	印　张：13.75
版　次：2022 年 4 月第 1 版	印　次：2022 年 4 月第 1 次印刷
字　数：200 千字	定　价：138.00 元

ISBN 978-7-5130-7757-6

编委会

供稿单位

河北省知识产权局 山西省知识产权局
辽宁省知识产权局 吉林省知识产权局
黑龙江省知识产权局 江苏省知识产权局
浙江省知识产权局 安徽省知识产权局
福建省知识产权局 江西省知识产权局
山东省知识产权局 河南省知识产权局
湖北省知识产权局 湖南省知识产权局
广东省知识产权局 广西壮族自治区知识产权局
海南省知识产权局 重庆市知识产权局
四川省知识产权局 贵州省知识产权局
云南省知识产权局 甘肃省知识产权局
宁夏回族自治区知识产权局
新疆维吾尔自治区知识产权局

目录

CONTENTS

咖啡

花卉

中药材

肉、蛋、乳及其制品

水产品及其制品

酒类

地理标志涉外保护概况

中国政府高度重视知识产权保护工作。习近平主席指出，“加强知识产权保护。这是完善产权保护制度最重要的内容，也是提高中国经济竞争力最大的激励”。地理标志作为重要的知识产权类型，对于提升产品品质、提高市场竞争力、提高附加值、增加生产者收入、保障消费者权益以及传承文化遗产等都具有重要意义。《中华人民共和国民法典》已将地理标志明文列入，作为重要的知识产权进行保护。

2018 年新一轮国家机构改革后，国家知识产权局负责地理标志保护工作，承担地理标志登记注册和行政裁决，拟定统一认定制度并组织实施，这是我国推进治理体系和治理能力现代化的重要举措，为高效保护和管理地理标志奠定了体制机制基础。当前，地理标志数量稳步提升，地理标志生产者市场主体数量持续增加、规模不断扩大。

截至 2021 年 12 月底，中国累计批准地理标志产品 2490 个，地理标志作为集体商标和证明商标注册 6562 件；累计核准地理标志专用标志使用市场主体 17111 家，数量持续增加、规模不断扩大。中欧双方通过单独申请、试点互认和协定互保等模式累计实现 110 个中国地理标志在欧保护，134 个欧盟地理标志在华保护。

The Chinese government has attached great importance to the protection of intellectual property rights. President Xi Jinping pointed out that "IPR protection is the centerpiece of the system for improving property rights protection, and it would provide the biggest boost to enhancing the competitiveness of the Chinese economy". As an important form of intellectual property, geographical indications are of great significance for improving product quality, improving market competitiveness, increasing added value, increasing incomes of the producer, safeguarding consumers' rights and interests, and inheriting the cultural heritage. The geographical indication was included in the scope of protection of the *Civil Code of the People's Republic of China* as an important form of intellectual property.

After the new round of national institutional reform in 2018, the CNIPA took charge of the protection of geographical indications, managed the registration of geographical indications and the issuance of administrative rulings, formulated a unified system of right affirmation, and saw it implemented. This was an important measure for China to promote the modernization of the governance system and governance capabilities, which laid the foundation of the regime for the efficient protection and administration of geographical indications. The number of geographical indications has been steadily increasing, the number of market entities of geographical indication producers has kept a continuous growth, and expanding industrial communities have come into shape.

As of the end of September 2021, a total of 2,490 geographical indication products have been approved in China, and 6,562 geographical indications have been registered as collective trademarks and certification trademarks. A total of 17,111 market entities have been entitled to the use of special marks of geographical indications, and this community has continued to expand. China and the European Union (EU) have implemented the protection of 110 Chinese geographical indications in Europe and 134 EU geographical indications in China through such channels as separate applications, mutual recognition pilots, and mutual protection agreements.

Special Sign for Geographical Indication

地理标志专用标志

2019 年 10 月 16 日，国家知识产权局发布地理标志专用标志官方标志。国家知识产权局对地理标志专用标志予以登记备案，并纳入官方标志保护。原相关地理标志产品专用标志同时废止，使用过渡期至 2020 年 12 月 31 日。

地理标志专用标志以经纬线地球为基底，表现了地理标志作为全球通行的一种知识产权类别和地理标志助推中国产品“走出去”的美好愿景。以长城及山峦剪影为前景，兼顾地理与人文的双重意象，代表着中国地理标志的卓越品质与可靠性，透明镂空的设计增强了标志在不同产品包装背景下的融合度与适应性。水稻源于中国，是中国最具代表性的农产品之一，标志上的稻穗象征着丰收。标志上的中文为“中华人民共和国地理标志”，英文为“GEOGRAPHICAL INDICATION OF P.R.CHINA”，均采用华文宋体。“GI”为国际通用的“Geographical Indication”的缩写名称，采用华文黑体。标志整体庄重大方，构图合理美观，体现了官方标志的权威，象征着中国传统的深厚底蕴，作为地理标志专用标志，具有较高的辨识度和较强的象征性。

On October 16, 2019, the CNIPA published the official design of the special sign for geographical indications. The CNIPA shall register and record the use of the special sign for geographical indications and include it in the protection of official signs. The former design of the special sign for geographical indication products shall be abolished, and a transition period where the former and the current versions are both allowable in use was terminated on December 31, 2020.

In the special sign for geographical indications, a pattern of the earth outlined by the latitude and longitude lines serves as the background, indicating that geographical indication is a form of intellectual property protected globally, and expressing a good vision that geographical indications may help Chinese products "go global". The Great Wall and a silhouette of a hill are taken as the foreground, taking into account both the relevance to geography and humanity, and embodying the excellent quality and reliability of Chinese geographical indications. The transparent hollow-out design enhances the adaptability of the sign to different backgrounds of product packaging. Rice, one of the most representative agricultural products in China, is an image originating from the Chinese culture, the ear of rice symbolizes a bumper harvest. The Chinese characters, i.e., “中华人民共和国地理标志”, and their English counterparts, i.e., "GEOGRAPHICAL INDICATION OF P. R. CHINA", are both printed in the Chinese Song style. "GI" is the international abbreviation of "Geographical Indication", printed in the Chinese boldface style. The overall design looks classic and grand, embodies the authority of the officials in a proper composition, and symbolizes the heritage of Chinese tradition. As the special sign for geographical indications, this design has high differentiation degree and profound connotation.

Introduction of *Agreement Between the Government of the People's Republic of China and the European Union on Cooperation on, and Protection of Geographical Indications*

《中华人民共和国政府与欧洲联盟地理标志保护与合作协定》简介

《中华人民共和国政府与欧洲联盟地理标志保护与合作协定》（下称《中欧地理标志协定》）于2011年启动谈判，历经8年22轮正式谈判和多轮非正式磋商，于2019年年底结束。2020年9月14日，中欧双方正式签署《中欧地理标志协定》。《中欧地理标志协定》具有保护数量多、保护种类丰富、保护待遇高的三大特点，是中国对外商签的第一个全面的、高水平的地理标志保护双边协定。

2021年3月1日，《中欧地理标志协定》正式生效，第一批100个中国产品同步在欧盟全境获得地理标志保护，《中欧地理标志协定》实施工作迈出坚实的一步。未来四年，中国将与欧盟共同推进第二批“175+175”中欧清单产品互认互保的技术准备工作。

接下来，中国国家知识产权局将会同有关方面进一步完善地理标志保护体系，深化地理标志管理改革，推动地理标志高水平保护、高标准管理、高质量发展。

The negotiations on the *Agreement Between the Government of the People's Republic of China and the European Union on Cooperation on, and Protection of Geographical Indications* (the "*China-EU Agreement on Geographical Indications*") started in 2011 and ended at the end of 2019. After 8 years through 22 rounds of formal negotiations and informal consultations, on September 14, 2020, China and the EU formally signed the *China-EU Agreement on Geographical Indications*. The *China-EU Agreement on Geographical Indications* includes a large number of products into protection, covers a wide range of categories, and provides a high-level treatment. This is the first comprehensive and high-level bilateral treaty on geographical indications which is negotiated and signed by China with foreign countries.

On March 1, 2021, the *China-EU Agreement on Geographical Indications* came into effect. The first batch of 100 Chinese products were simultaneously protected as geographical indications across the EU, which was a solid step forward in the performance of the *China-EU Agreement on Geographical Indications*. In the next four years, China and the EU will jointly carry forward the work of technical preparations for the second batch of "175+175" products on the list under the Agreement.

The CNIPA will promptly work with relevant parties to further improve the regime of geographical indication protection, deepen the reform of geographical indication administration, and promote the protection, administration, and development of geographical indications to a higher level.

Product Catalog of China Geographical Indication Products refer to *Agreement Between the Government of the People's Republic of China and the European Union on Cooperation on, and Protection of Geographical Indications*（First batch）

《中华人民共和国政府与欧洲联盟地理标志保护与合作协定》原产于中国的地理标志产品名录（第一批）

	在中华人民共和国注册的名称	拉丁字母意译
1	安吉白茶	Anji White Tea
2	安溪铁观音	Anxi Tie Guan Yin
3	保山小粒咖啡	Baoshan Arabica Coffee
4	赣南脐橙	Gannan Navel Orange
5	霍山黄芽	Huoshan Yellow Bud Tea
6	郫县豆瓣	Pixian Bean Paste
7	普洱茶	Pu'er Tea
8	山西老陈醋	Shanxi Aged Vinegar
9	烟台苹果	Yantai Apple
10	坦洋工夫	Tanyang Gongfu Black Tea
11	白城绿豆	Baicheng Mung Bean
12	肇源大米	Zhaoyuan Rice
13	婺源绿茶	Wuyuan Green Tea
14	福州茉莉花茶	Fuzhou Jasmine Tea

	在中华人民共和国注册的名称	拉丁字母意译
15	房县香菇	Fangxian Mushroom
16	南丰蜜桔	Nanfeng Sweet Orange
17	苍山大蒜	Cangshan Garlic
18	房县黑木耳	Fangxian Black Fungus
19	凤冈锌硒茶	Fenggang Zinc Selenium Tea
20	库尔勒香梨	Korla Pear
21	邳州大蒜	Pizhou Garlic
22	安岳柠檬	Anyue Lemon
23	正山小种	Lapsang Souchong
24	兴化香葱	Xinghua Chive
25	六安瓜片	Lu'an Melon-seed-shaped Tea
26	宜宾芽菜	Yibin Bean Sprout
27	静宁苹果	Jingning Apple
28	安丘大姜	Anqiu Ginger

	在中华人民共和国注册的名称	拉丁字母意译
29	建宁通心白莲	Jianning White Lotus Nut
30	松溪绿茶	Songxi Green Tea
31	罗平小黄姜	Luoping Yellow Ginger
32	苍溪红心猕猴桃	Cangxi Red Kiwi Fruit
33	庆元香菇	Qingyuan Mushroom
34	长寿沙田柚	Changshou Shantian Pomelo
35	凤凰单丛	Fenghuang Single Cluster
36	涪城麦冬	Fucheng *Ophiopogon japonicus*
37	狗牯脑	Gougunao Tea
38	武夷山大红袍	Mount Wuyi Da Hong Pao
39	晋州鸭梨	Jinzhou Pear
40	吐鲁番葡萄干	Turpan Raisin
41	安化黑茶	Anhua Dark Tea
42	嵊泗贻贝	Shengsi Mussel
43	辽中玫瑰	Liaozhong Rose
44	横县茉莉花茶	Hengxian Jasmine Tea
45	蒲江雀舌	Pujiang Que She Tea
46	峨眉山茶	Mount Emei Tea
47	朵贝茶	Duobei Tea
48	五常大米	Wuchang Rice

	在中华人民共和国注册的名称	拉丁字母意译
49	福鼎白茶	Fuding White Tea
50	吴川月饼	Wuchuan Mooncake
51	兴隆咖啡	Xinglong Coffee
52	绍兴酒	Shaoxing Rice Wine
53	贺兰山东麓葡萄酒	Wine in Helan Mountain East Region
54	桓仁冰酒	Huanren Icewine
55	烟台葡萄酒	Yantai Wine
56	惠水黑糯米酒	Huishui Black Glutinous Rice Wine
57	西峡香菇	Xixia Mushroom
58	红崖子花生	Hongyazi Peanut
59	武夷岩茶	Wuyi Rock Tea
60	英德红茶	Yingde Black Tea
61	剑南春酒	Jian Nan Chun Liquor
62	高炉家酒（高炉酒）	Gao Lu Jia Liquor/ Gao Lu Liquor
63	扳倒井酒	Ban Dao Jing Liquor
64	沙城葡萄酒	Shacheng Wine
65	茅台酒（贵州茅台酒）	Moutai Liquor/ Kweichow Moutai Liquor
66	五粮液	Wuliangye Liquor
67	盘锦大米	Panjin Rice

	在中华人民共和国注册的名称	拉丁字母意译
68	吉县苹果	Jixian Apple
69	鄂托克阿尔巴斯山羊肉	Otog Arbas Goat Meat
70	扎兰屯黑木耳	Zhalantun Black Fungus
71	岫岩滑子蘑	Xiuyan Pholiota Nameko
72	东港大黄蚬	Donggang Surf Clam
73	东宁黑木耳	Dongning Black Fungus
74	南京盐水鸭	Nanjing Salted Duck
75	千岛银珍	Qiandao Rare Tea
76	泰顺三杯香茶	Taishun Three Cups of Incense Tea
77	金华两头乌猪	Jinhua Pig
78	罗源秀珍菇	Luoyuan *Pleurotus* Geesteranus
79	桐江鲈鱼	Tongjiang Bass
80	乐安竹笋	Le'an Bamboo Shoots
81	莒南花生	Junan Peanut
82	文登苹果	Wendeng Apple
83	安丘大葱	Anqiu Chinese Onion

	在中华人民共和国注册的名称	拉丁字母意译
84	香花辣椒	Xianghua Chilli
85	麻城福白菊	Macheng Chrysanthemum Tea
86	潜江龙虾	Qianjiang Crayfish
87	宜都宜红茶	Yidu Black Tea
88	大埔蜜柚	Tai Po Honey Pomelo
89	桂平西山茶	Guiping Xishan Tea
90	百色芒果	Baise Mango
91	巫溪洋芋	Wuxi Potato
92	四川泡菜	Sichuan Style Pickles
93	纳溪特早茶	Naxi Early-Spring Tea
94	普洱咖啡	Pu'er Coffee
95	横山大明绿豆	Hengshan Daming Mung Bean
96	眉县猕猴桃	Meixian Kiwifruit
97	天祝白牦牛	Tianzhu White Yak
98	柴达木枸杞	Chaidamu Goji Berry
99	宁夏大米	Ningxia Rice
100	精河枸杞	Jinghe Goji Berry

Product Introduction of China Geographical Indication Products refer to *Agreement Between the Government of the People's Republic of China and the European Union on Cooperation on, and Protection of Geographical Indications*（First batch）

《中华人民共和国政府与欧洲联盟地理标志保护与合作协定》原产于中国的地理标志产品介绍（第一批）

Anji White Tea (or Anji Bai Cha) is a green tea, and its name was derived from its origin in Anji County, Zhejiang Province. Anji White Tea has delicate buds and leaves, one bud with one leaf or two or three leaves, resembling chicken feathers, in emerald green and yellow colors, bright and oily. The brewed tea has a fresh and lasting aroma, as well as delicate tea grounds like flowers, and each leaf is in white color with green veins. Anji White Tea is rich in a variety of amino acids desirable to human health, 3-4 times higher than those of ordinary green teas, but has fewer tea polyphenols than ordinary green teas, as a result, Anji White Tea looks clear and bright, has a fresh and pleasant taste without bitterness.

GI Profile

Notice Date: April 6, 2004

Producing Area: The administrative area of Anji County, Huzhou City, Zhejiang Province.

安吉白茶

Anji White Tea

安吉白茶属绿茶类，因产于浙江安吉而得名。安吉白茶芽叶细嫩，一芽一叶到二三叶，形似凤羽，色泽翠绿间黄，光亮油润，香气清鲜持久，叶底芽叶细嫩成朵，叶白脉翠。安吉白茶拥有人体所需的多种氨基酸，其含量高于普通绿茶 3—4 倍，且茶多酚含量低于普通绿茶，因而安吉白茶汤色清澈明亮，滋味鲜爽，没有苦涩味。

地理标志概况

公告日期：2004 年 4 月 6 日

产地范围：浙江省湖州市安吉县现辖行政区域。

Anxi County is the hometown of Chinese oolong teas and the birthplace of Tieguanyin, a tea renowned in the world. Anxi Tie Guan Yin, representative of oolong teas, is honored one of the top ten teas in China, famous for its unique "Guanyin flavor". The leaf has an oily black color and gloss, and a shape like a thick twisted strip, curly and compact, heavy like metal, and looks like a head of a green dragonfly. The brewed tea shines in a golden color, has a far-reaching sweet fragrance, and tastes mellow and fresh. Therefore, Anxi Tie Guan Yin has always enjoyed the reputation of "beautiful red-rimmed green leaves, and lingering fragrance even brewed for seven rounds".

GI Profile

Notice Date: July 8, 2004

Producing Area: The administrative area of Anxi County, Fujian Province.

安溪铁观音

Anxi Tie Guan Yin

安溪，中国乌龙茶之乡，世界名茶铁观音的发源地。安溪铁观音是中国十大名茶之一，乌龙茶类的代表，以独有的『观音韵』著称于世。产品色泽乌润，条索肥壮、卷曲紧实、沉重似铁，具有『青蒂绿腹蜻蜓头』的外形，汤色金黄明亮，香气清新悠长，滋味醇厚甘鲜，素有『绿叶红镶边，七泡有余香』之美誉。

地理标志概况

公告日期：2004 年 7 月 8 日

产地范围：福建省安溪县现辖行政区域。

Huoshan Yellow Bud Tea is a famous tea with a long history. As early as in the Tang Dynasty, the *Supplements to the Official History* recorded that "there are plenty of varieties of famous and precious tea, among them, Huoshan Yellow Bud Tea in the Shouzhou Prefecture stands out". Huoshan Yellow Bud Tea takes advantage of the superior geographical condition, the monsoon climate, proper sunshine, and abundant rainfall. The leaf has a straightened and slightly unfolded shape, resembles a bird's tongue, and has a greenish yellow color and fuzzy appearance. The brewed tea looks clear and transparent in a greenish yellow color, has a faint and lasting fragrance, and has a mellow flavor which turns from bitterness to sweetness, with tea grounds shining in a light yellow color.

GI Profile

Notice Date: April 16, 2006

Producing Area: The administrative area of Huoshan County, Anhui Province.

霍山黄芽

Huoshan Yellow Bud Tea

霍山黄芽为历史悠久的中国名茶。唐代《国史补》记载：『风俗贵茶，茶之名品益众……寿州有霍山之黄芽』。在优越的地理环境、季风气候条件、合适的光照及充沛的雨水滋润下，霍山黄芽外形挺直微展、形似雀舌，色泽黄绿披毫，汤色黄绿明亮，香气清香持久，滋味鲜醇回甘，叶底嫩黄鲜亮。

地理标志概况

公告日期：2006 年 4 月 16 日

产地范围：安徽省霍山县现辖行政区域。

Pu'er Tea has a long history, first appeared in the Shang and Zhou Dynasties, gained its popularity in the Han and Jin Dynasties, developed in the Tang and Song Dynasties, and flourished in the Ming and Qing Dynasties. Pu'er Tea is mainly made from Yunnan Big Leaf Shaiqing green tea and processed through a specific process, including raw tea and processed tea. The raw tea has a dark green color, a pure and lasting fragrance, strong and sweet flavor, and the brewed tea shines in a greenish yellow gloss; the processed tea experiences fermentation, has a reddish brown color, and its brewed tea is in bright red, with a rich and unique aroma and a mellow taste that turns from bitterness to sweetness.

GI Profile

Notice Date: May 13, 2008

Producing Area: The administrative area of 11 prefectures (cities), 75 counties (cities, districts), and 639 townships (towns, sub-districts), including Pu'er City, Xishuangbanna Prefecture, Lincang City, Kunming City, Dali Prefecture, Baoshan City, Dehong Prefecture, Chuxiong Prefecture, Honghe Prefecture, Yuxi City, and Wenshan Prefecture of Yunnan Province.

普洱茶

Pu'er Tea

普洱茶历史悠久，最早出现于商周时期，兴起于汉晋，发展于唐宋，鼎盛于明清。普洱茶主要以云南大叶种晒青茶为原料，采用特定工艺制成，分为生茶和熟茶两种类型。生茶外形色泽墨绿，香气清纯持久，滋味浓厚回甘，汤色绿黄清亮；熟茶经过发酵加工，外形色泽红褐，汤色红浓明亮，香气浓郁独特，滋味醇厚回甘。

地理标志概况

公告日期：2008 年 5 月 13 日

产地范围：云南省普洱市、西双版纳州、临沧市、昆明市、大理州、保山市、德宏州、楚雄州、红河州、玉溪市、文山州 11 个州（市）、75 个县（市、区）、639 个乡（镇、街道办事处）现辖行政区域。

Tanyang Gongfu Black Tea was created in 1851, and won the gold award at the 1915 Panama Pacific International Exposition, enjoying a worldwide reputation. The process and skills for making Tanyang Gongfu Black Tea are complex, and the process includes "fading, kneading, leavening, baking, shaking, separating, collecting, selecting, trashing, and bleaching". As such, the processed leaf has the shape like a tight and thin strip, with golden hairs, neat, clean, in an oily black color. The brewed tea has a rich fruity fragrance, tastes fresh and mellow, and shines in an red color, with soft and graceful tea grounds.

GI Profile

Notice Date: February 14, 2007

Producing Area: The administrative area of Fu'an City, Fujian Province.

坦洋工夫

Tanyang Gongfu Black Tea

坦洋工夫茶创制于1851年，1915年曾获巴拿马万国博览会金奖，享誉全球。『坦洋工夫』的技艺复杂，有『萎、揉、酵、烘、抖、分、捞、选、簸、漂』十大核心工艺，成品条索紧细、有金毫显锋苗、匀整、洁净，色泽乌黑油润；香气甜香浓郁、带花果香，滋味鲜浓醇爽，汤色红艳明亮；叶底细嫩柔软、红亮。

地理标志概况

公告日期：2007年2月14日

产地范围：福建省福安市现辖行政区域。

Wuyuan Green Tea, abbreviated as "Wu Lv", is produced in Wuyuan County, Jiangxi Province. Wuyuan has a long history of producing teas, as early as in the Tang Dynasty, Wuyuan tea was recorded in the *Classic of Tea*, ranked the top in its kind in the Song Dynasty, and became a royal tribute in the Ming and Qing Dynasties. The plant of Wuyuan Green Tea has soft leaves which feature good freshness, with fat buds and thick leaves, known for its "green and natural color, fragrant and rich aftertaste, and refreshing and mellow flavor when brewed", suitable for making high-quality green tea. Required by the traditional techniques, it is preferably one bud plus one leaf that should be picked; after the Pure Brightness, it is one bud plus two leaves that should be picked.

GI Profile

Notice Date: October 31, 2008

Producing Area: The administrative area of Wuyuan County, Shangrao City, Jiangxi Province.

婺源绿茶

Wuyuan Green Tea

婺源绿茶，简称『婺绿』，产于江西省婺源县。婺源产茶历史悠久，唐载茶经、宋称绝品、明清入贡。婺源绿茶叶质柔软，持嫩性好，芽肥叶厚，素以『颜色碧而天然，回味香而浓郁，水叶清而润厚』的品质著称，宜制优质绿茶。婺源绿茶采用传统手工加工工艺采摘时，按一芽一叶标准；清明后，按一芽二叶标准。

地理标志概况

公告日期：2008 年 10 月 31 日

产地范围：江西省上饶市婺源县现辖行政区域。

Fuzhou Jasmine Tea, with a history of nearly a thousand years, originated in Fuzhou City. Fuzhou Jasmine Tea is a reprocessed tea made by mixing processed and dried tea-leaves with jasmine flowers in early puberty and then scenting the mixture, and generally taking green tea as the tea base, sometimes, taking black tea and oolong tea instead. The brewed tea has a fresh and lasting fragrance and a mellow and refreshing flavor, shining in greenish yellow, with tea grounds being soft and in light color.

GI Profile

Notice Date: January 6, 2008

Producing Area: 5 districts and 8 counties (cities) in the administrative areas of Fuzhou City, Fujian Province, including Changle City, Fuqing City, Minhou County, Lianjiang County, Luoyuan County, Yongtai County, Minqing County, Pingtan County, Cangshan District, Jin'an District , Mawei District, Taijiang District, and Gulou District; the producing area of Fuzhou jasmine is the both banks of the lower reaches of Minjiang River and the counties (cities) of Minjiang River estuary.

福州茉莉花茶

Fuzhou Jasmine Tea

福州是茉莉花茶的发源地，已有近千年历史。福州茉莉花茶是用经加工干燥的茶叶，与含苞待放的茉莉鲜花混合窨制而成的再加工茶，通常以绿茶为茶坯，少数也用红茶和乌龙茶；其香气鲜灵持久，滋味醇厚鲜爽，汤色黄绿明亮，叶底嫩匀柔软。

地理标志概况

公告日期：2008年1月6日

产地范围：福建省福州市行政区内五区八县（市），即长乐市、福清市、闽侯县、连江县、罗源县、永泰县、闽清县、平潭县、仓山区、晋安区、马尾区、台江区、鼓楼区；福州茉莉花的生产区域范围为闽江下游两岸及闽江口的县（市）区。

The *Classics of Tea*, written by Lu Yu in the Tang Dynasty, recorded that this tea, originating in Guizhou, has been grown in Sizhou, Bozhou, Feizhou, and Yizhou prefectures, and its taste was excellent, where Yizhou is Fenggang County today. Fenggang is located in the industrial area to produce famous and upmarket teas in China, near 30 degrees north latitude. The brewed tea shines in a greenish yellow color, tastes crisp and not puckery, strong but without bitterness, with freshness mixed in mellowness and lingering sweetness, and smells refreshing. This tea is unique for its high content of zinc and selenium. The leaf is evenly shaped and compact, oily in color, and can keep its long-lasting fragrance after even several rounds of brewing.

GI Profile

Notice Date: January 24, 2006

Producing Area: The administrative area of Fenggang County, Guizhou Province.

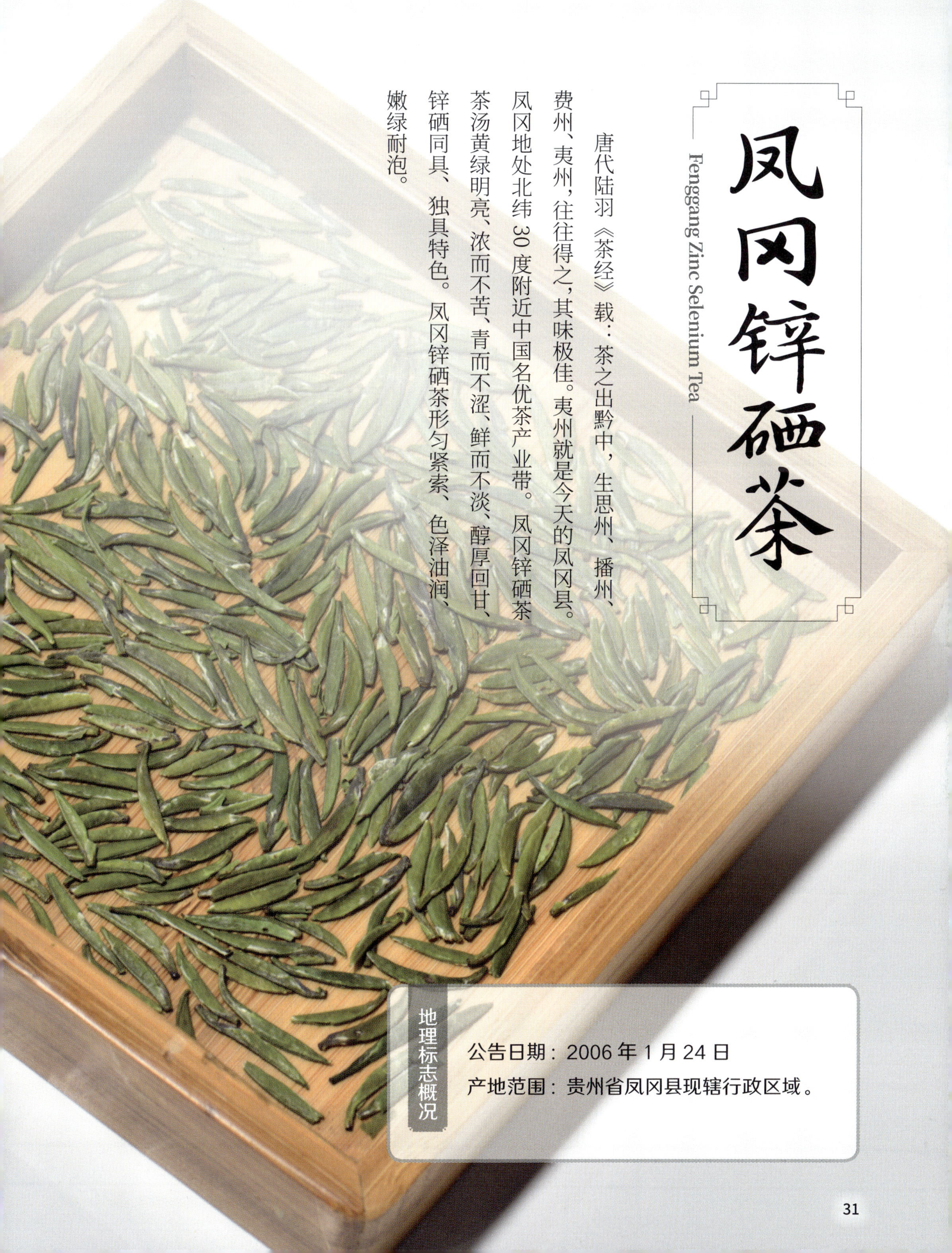

凤冈锌硒茶

Fenggang Zinc Selenium Tea

唐代陆羽《茶经》载：茶之出黔中，生思州、播州、费州、夷州，往往得之，其味极佳。夷州就是今天的凤冈县。凤冈地处北纬 30 度附近中国名优茶产业带。凤冈锌硒茶茶汤黄绿明亮、浓而不苦、青而不涩、鲜而不淡、醇厚回甘、锌硒同具，独具特色。凤冈锌硒茶形匀紧索，色泽油润、嫩绿耐泡。

地理标志概况

公告日期：2006 年 1 月 24 日

产地范围：贵州省凤冈县现辖行政区域。

Growing in the Mount Wuyi (or Wuyi Mountains), which is the birthplace of the black tea, Lapsang Souchong (or Zhengshan Xiao Zhong Tea) is the earliest ancestor of black teas and has a history of more than 400 years. As a world natural heritage site, Mount Wuyi has mild climate, abundant rainfall, high humidity, and perennial mist. Therefore, Lapsang Souchong grows in a especially favorable natural environment, and the tea trees grow at an average elevation of 1000-1200 meters. Lapsang Souchong is a fully-fermented black tea, has a shape like a twisted strip, in a oily black color. The brewed tea has a dark red color and a far-reaching fragrance like that of pine soot, tastes mellow, with the flavor of the longan soup.

GI Profile

Notice Date: January 13, 2010

Producing Area: 11 townships (towns), subdistricts, and farms including Xingcun Town, Wuyi Subdistrict, Xingtian Town, Wufu Town, Chong'an Town, Yangzhuang Township, Langu Township, Shangmei Township, Wutun Township, Xinfeng Subdistrict, and Comprehensive Farms of the administrative area of Mount Wuyi, Fujian Province.

正山小种

Lapsang Souchong

武夷山是世界红茶的发源地。正山小种是世界上较早的红茶，至今已有400多年的历史，生长在『世界自然遗产地』武夷山，自然气候独一无二，气温低、降水多、湿度大、雾日长，茶树生长的平均海拔为1000—1200米。正山小种属全发酵红茶，外形条索肥实，色泽乌润，泡水后汤色红浓，香气高长带松烟香，滋味醇厚，带有桂圆汤味。

地理标志概况

公告日期：2010年1月13日

产地范围：福建省武夷山行政区划内的星村镇、武夷街道、兴田镇、五夫镇、崇安镇、洋庄乡、岚谷乡、上梅乡、吴屯乡、新丰街道、综合农场共11个乡（镇）、街道、农场。

The history of Lu'an Melon-seed-shaped Tea can date back to long ago. As early as in the Tang Dynasty, the *Classic of Tea*, written by Lu Yu, recorded "Lu'an Tea of Luzhou Prefecture". In the Ming Dynasty, Xu Guangqi, acclaimed in his *Agricultural Encyclopedia* that "laminar tea from Lu'an Prefecture is a top-grade tea".

Each leaf is in a single piece, flat and oval, resembling a melon seed, with the edge of the leaf curling up slightly. The leaf has a crystal green color and a regular shape. The tea has a faint and pleasant scent, and a mellow flavor which turns from bitterness to sweetness. The brewed tea looks clear and transparent, with tea grounds shining in a light green color. This tea is preferably picked within the Grain Rain each year, one bud plus one leaf, and the fully grown ones are more prioritized than the fresh ones. This tea has been honored as one of the top ten teas in China.

GI Profile

Notice Date: December 28, 2007

Producing Area: The administrative areas of 26 townships in 5 districts and counties including Yu'an District, Jinzhai County, Huoshan County, Jin'an District, and Shucheng County of Lu'an City, Anhui Province.

安瓜片

on-seed-shaped Tea

史悠久。唐代陆羽《茶经》
茶）』之称。明代徐光启在《农
安州之片茶，为茶之极品』。
，外观形似瓜子、自然平展，
宝绿，大小匀整，清香高爽，
汤色清澈透亮，叶底绿嫩明
后十天内采摘，取一芽一叶，
嫩』，为中国十大名茶之一。

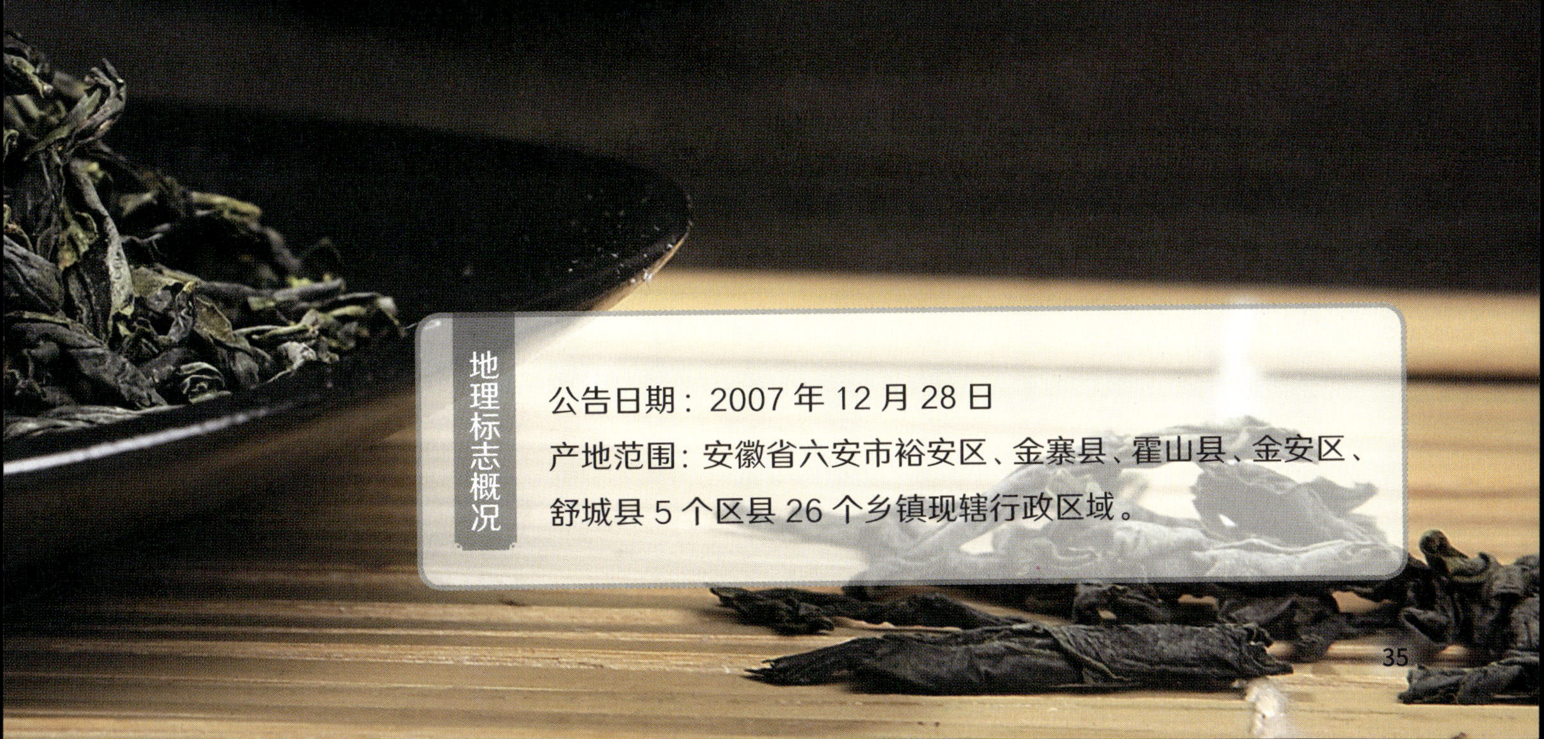

地理标志概况

公告日期：2007 年 12 月 28 日

产地范围：安徽省六安市裕安区、金寨县、霍山县、金安区、舒城县 5 个区县 26 个乡镇现辖行政区域。

Songxi Green Tea has a long history, and has been a tribute tea for generations since the Northern Song Dynasty. Songxi Green Tea features dried tea-leaves processed by subjecting high-quality tea-leaves to steaming, stir-frying, and baking, and deactivating the enzyme under a high temperature. The dried tea-leaves have bud-like, flat, curved, and strip shapes, etc. The tea leaf has a beautiful appearance and a green color. The brewed tea shines in a yellowish green color, has a rich and mellow flavor, with oily and fresh tea grounds, and the refreshing fragrance and pleasant flavor last even after several times of brewing.

GI Profile

Notice Date: May 27, 2009

Producing Area: 9 townships (towns) including Songyuan Town, Hedong Township, Jiuxian Township, Weitian Town, Xidong Township, Zhengdun Town, Huaqiao Township, Zudun Township, and Chaping Township in the administrative area of Songxi County, Nanping City, Fujian Province.

松溪绿茶

Songxi Green Tea

松溪绿茶历史悠久，自北宋起就是历代贡茶。

松溪绿茶采用优质茶青，以蒸、炒、烘等工艺，通过高温使酶活性钝化，制成芽形、扁形、曲形、条形等形状的干茶。其外形秀美，色泽绿润，汤色黄绿明亮，滋味浓厚，叶底肥嫩，香高味爽耐冲泡。

地理标志概况

公告日期：2009 年 5 月 27 日

产地范围：福建省南平市松溪县行政区内的松源镇、河东乡、旧县乡、渭田镇、溪东乡、郑墩镇、花桥乡、祖墩乡、茶坪乡 9 个乡镇。

Tea production in Chaozhou can date back to 900 years ago. The tea grown on these plants was subjected to individual tea-picking, individual processing, and individual sales. The name "Fenghuang Single Cluster" derives from its origin in Fenghuang Mountain of Chaozhou City. Fenghuang Single Cluster has a reputation of "indispensable fragrance and flavor to its individual character", has a natural floral fragrance that lasts for long, tastes mellow and fresh, and turns from bitterness to lingering sweetness. It has a special plant flavor and a honey flavor, and induces a special mountain-related artistic conception. The brewed tea remains tasteful still after many rounds of brewing.

GI Profile

Notice Date: April 6, 2010

Producing Area: The northern, eastern, and central areas of the administrative area of Chaozhou City, Guangdong Province, including: Fenghuang Town, Tiepu Town, Wenci Town, Linxi Town, Guantang Town, Dengtang Town, Chifeng Town, Guihu Town, Guxiang Town, Fengtang Town, and Wanfeng Forest Farm of Chao'an County; Fubin Town, Qiandong Town, Zhangxi Town, Fushan Town, Tangxi Town, Sanrao Town, Lianrao Town, Xinxu Town, Xinfeng Town, Raoyang Town, Shangrao Town, Jianrao Town, Gaotang Town, Xintang Town, and Dongshan Town of Raoping County; Yixi Town and Qiaodong Subdistrict Tea Area of Xiangqiao District; Yunbu Caolanwu and Huaishangang Tea Area of Fengxi District.

凤凰单丛

Fenghuang Single Cluster

潮州产茶历史久远，至今已有900多年历史。潮州茶实行单株采摘、单株制茶、单株销售，由于发源于潮州凤凰山，因此又称『凤凰单丛（枞）茶』。凤凰单丛（枞）茶有『无香不成单、无韵不成单』的美誉，具有天然自然花香，悠长清雅，浓醇鲜爽，回甘持久，有特殊丛韵味、蜜韵味和特殊山韵，极耐冲泡。

地理标志概况

公告日期：2010 年 4 月 6 日

产地范围：广东省潮州市行政辖区的北部、东部和中部地区。具体包括：潮安县的凤凰镇、铁铺镇、文祠镇、磷溪镇、官塘镇、登塘镇、赤凤镇、归湖镇、古巷镇、凤塘镇、万峰林场；饶平县的浮滨镇、钱东镇、樟溪镇、浮山镇、汤溪镇、三饶镇、联饶镇、新圩镇、新丰镇、饶洋镇、上饶镇、建饶镇、高堂镇、新塘镇、东山镇；湘桥区的意溪镇、桥东街道茶区；枫溪区的云步草岚武、槐山岗茶区。

Gougunao Tea was first produced in the first year of the reign of Emperor Jiaqing in the Qing Dynasty. Its name was derived from its origin in Gougunao Mountain in Tanghu Town, Suichuan County, Jiangxi Province, at the southern foot of Jinggang Mountain in the Luoxiao Mountains.

The leaf has a compact shape, a green color, and a faint aroma. The brewed tea has a bright color, a sweet taste, with fresh tea grounds. An exquisite process is required in tea-picking and preparation. Generally, tea-picking takes place in mid-to-late March. A high-grade leaf-freshness standard requires that one bud or one bud plus one leaf having just unfolded should be picked. Tea farmers don't pick dewed and rained leaves, or pick leaves at the noon on sunny days. The picked fresh leaves are screened to remove purple bud leaves, single-piece leaves and fish leaves (the leaf lower than the bud and unfolding leaf).

GI Profile

Notice Date: January 29, 2004

Producing Area: The administrative area of Suichuan County, Jiangxi Province.

狗牯脑

Gougunao Tea

狗牯脑茶始产于清代嘉庆元年，因产于罗霄山脉井冈南麓江西省遂川县汤湖境内的狗牯脑山而得名。

狗牯脑茶外形紧结、色泽嫩绿、香气清雅、汤色明亮、滋味甘醇、叶底鲜活。其采制十分精细，一般在三月中下旬开采，鲜叶标准为一芽或一芽一叶初展。不采露水叶、雨水叶，晴天中午不采叶。鲜叶采回后先挑选，剔除紫芽叶、单片叶和鱼叶。

地理标志概况

公告日期：2004 年 1 月 29 日

产地范围：江西省遂川县现辖行政区域。

Originating in Mount Wuyi, Mount Wuyi Da Hong Pao is the best among oolong teas, and the process and skills for making this tea were included in the National Intangible Cultural Heritage List. Mount Wuyi Da Hong Pao is a semi-fermented oolong tea. The tea leaf, warm in nature, has a unique quality, and a rich flavor and fragrance which can endure long-term storage and several times of brewing. The fragrance may get more refreshing and the flavor may get even richer after a long preservation. Drinking this tea, you may feel "gentle flavor to keep up your spirits, and refreshing fragrance to clear your mind", and this feeling may linger and produce a unique "rock" flavor.

GI Profile

Notice Date: December 21, 2001

Producing Area: The specific natural environment of Wuyi Mountain Scenic Spot in Fujian Province, extends to Luotuo Peak in the east, Lingxiao Peak, Huxiao Rock, and Lanshi Peak in the west, Wuyi Palace in the south, and Sanyang Peak in the north.

武夷山大红袍

Mount Wuyi Da Hong Pao

武夷山是乌龙茶的发源地，武夷山大红袍是乌龙茶中的极品，其制作技艺被列入国家级非物质文化遗产名录。武夷山大红袍属半发酵的乌龙茶，品质独特，重味求香，性和不寒，耐藏耐泡，香久益清，味久益醇。饮后有『味轻醍醐，香薄兰芷』之感，舒适持久，具有独特的『岩韵』。

地理标志概况

公告日期：2001 年 12 月 21 日

产地范围：福建省武夷山景区特定的自然环境中，即东至骆驼峰，西至凌霄峰、虎啸岩、揽石峰，南至武夷宫，北至三仰峰。

Anhua County is one of the birthplaces of dark tea in China and has a relatively unique geographical environment and a climate that are very suitable for the growth of tea trees. The fresh leaves of Anhua Yuntai Large Leaf tea are taken as the raw materials for Anhua Dark Tea, and are processed through pile fermentation, baking with a seven-fire-hole stove, natural drying, and development of dominant microbes. The brewed tea is as bright as an amber, has a mellow taste, a pure aroma, and turns from bitterness to sweetness. The skills for processing Anhua Dark Tea have been recognized in the National Intangible Cultural Heritage List.

GI Profile

Notice Date: April 6, 2010

Producing Area: 32 townships (towns) including Qingtangpu Town, Meicheng Town, Le'an Town, Xianxi Town, Changtang Town, Dafu Town, Yangjiaotang Town, Lengshi Town, Longtang Township, Xiaoyan Town, Taoxi Town, Jiangnan Town, Tianzhuang Township, Dongping Town, Zhexi Town, Malu Town, Kuixi Town, Yanxi Town, Pingkou Town, Qujiang Town, Nanjin Township, and Gulou Township of Anhua County; Taohua Town, Shiniujiang Town, Fuqiushan Township, Lucidu Town, Daligang Town, and Majitang Town of Taojiang County; Xinshidu Town, Nijiangkou Town, and Cangshuipu Town of Heshan District, and Xinqiaohe Town of Ziyang District, Yiyang City, Hunan Province.

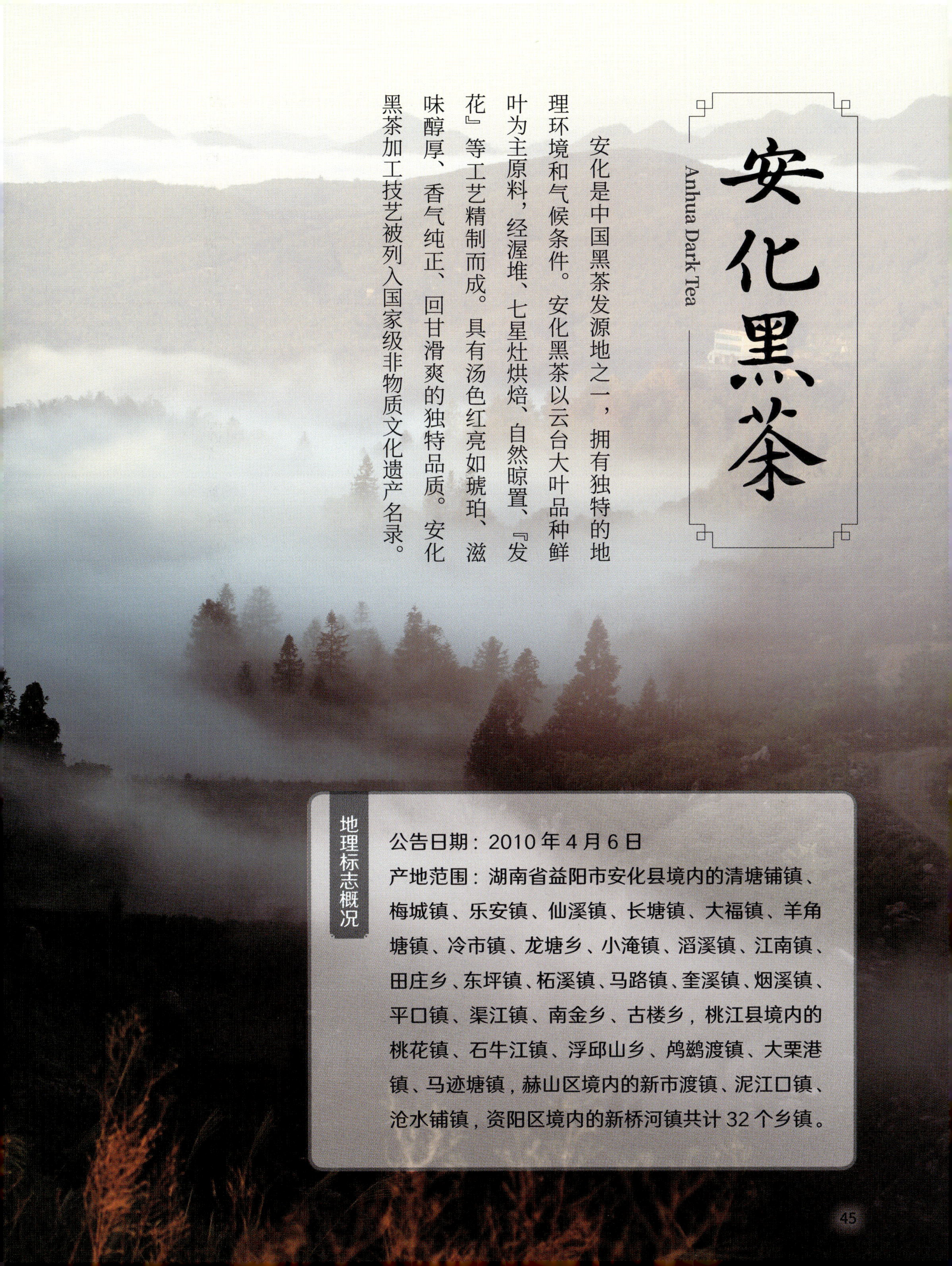

安化黑茶

Anhua Dark Tea

安化是中国黑茶发源地之一，拥有独特的地理环境和气候条件。安化黑茶以云台大叶品种鲜叶为主原料，经渥堆、七星灶烘焙、自然晾置、『发花』等工艺精制而成。具有汤色红亮如琥珀、滋味醇厚、香气纯正、回甘滑爽的独特品质。安化黑茶加工技艺被列入国家级非物质文化遗产名录。

地理标志概况

公告日期：2010 年 4 月 6 日

产地范围：湖南省益阳市安化县境内的清塘铺镇、梅城镇、乐安镇、仙溪镇、长塘镇、大福镇、羊角塘镇、冷市镇、龙塘乡、小淹镇、滔溪镇、江南镇、田庄乡、东坪镇、柘溪镇、马路镇、奎溪镇、烟溪镇、平口镇、渠江镇、南金乡、古楼乡，桃江县境内的桃花镇、石牛江镇、浮邱山乡、鸬鹚渡镇、大栗港镇、马迹塘镇，赫山区境内的新市渡镇、泥江口镇、沧水铺镇，资阳区境内的新桥河镇共计 32 个乡镇。

Hengxian County has a long history of jasmine plantation, and there has been a written record of jasmine plantation since the Ming Dynasty. Fertile soil, abundant sunshine, and a warm climate contribute to the highly recognized reputation of the jasmine of Hengxian County for its early appearance in the market, long blooming period, large buds, high yield, good quality, and rich fragrance. The processed tea-leaf, made from Hengxian jasmine, has a shape like slim and compact strips, which is aesthetic in its appearance, and has a rich aroma and lasting freshness. The brewed tea tastes mellow, with tender tea grounds, and the fragrance may still linger even after rounds of brewing.

GI Profile

Notice Date: December 12, 2013

Producing Area: The administrative area of Hengxian County, Guangxi Zhuang Autonomous Region.

横县茉莉花茶

Hengxian Jasmine Tea

横县茉莉花种植历史悠久，早在明代就有关于种植茉莉花的文字记录。肥沃的土壤、充足的阳光、温暖的气候，使得横县茉莉花以上市早、花期长、花蕾大、产量高、质量好、香味浓而闻名天下。用『横县茉莉花』窨制的『横县茉莉花茶』具有条索紧细、外形秀美、香气浓郁、鲜灵持久、滋味浓醇、叶底嫩匀、经久耐泡的优良品质。

地理标志概况

公告日期：2013 年 12 月 12 日

产地范围：广西壮族自治区横县现辖行政区域。

According to the *Book of Tea*, written by Mao Wenxi, a minister and a poet in the Later Shu Dynasty, several counties in Linqiong produce teas, including Huoqian tea, Huohou tea, Nenlv tea, and Huangya tea. "Huoqian" is the name of the tea, which refers to the fresh tea picked and processed before the Cold Food Festival, which is two days before the Qingming Festival. The name "Que She" was derived from the slim and uniform shape of its bud, resembling a bird tongue (pinyin: "Que She"). For more than a thousand years, this tea has followed the traditional techniques and inherited "green color, rich fragrance, mellow taste and beautiful appearance", favored by people.

GI Profile

Notice Date: October 31, 2008

Producing Area: The administrative area of Pujiang County, Sichuan Province.

蒲江雀舌

Pujiang Que She Tea

据后蜀大臣、词人毛文锡《茶谱》记载：临邛数邑茶，有火前、火后、嫩绿、黄芽号。『火前』即茶名，是指在清明前两日的寒食节之前采制而成的嫩茶，因其芽嫩细匀、细小，称为雀舌，『蒲江雀舌』便由此得名。蒲江雀舌茶千余年来沿袭传统工艺，传承了『色翠、香高、味醇、形美』的独特品质，深受人们喜爱和称颂。

地理标志概况

公告日期：2008 年 10 月 31 日

产地范围：四川省蒲江县现辖行政区域。

In the civilization development of the past 3,000 years in Leshan City, Mount Emei Tea and its tea culture have played a very important role and forged a colorful and profound cultural landscape together with Leshan Confucianism, Buddhism, and Taoism. Mount Emei Tea is green tea, it has flat, straight and smooth leaves in a light greenish and oily color, producing a far-reaching faint scent, pleasantly refreshing. The brewed tea smells pleasant and tastes mellow and sweet, rich in tea polyphenols, amino acids, vitamins and other nutrients, and thus enjoys a reputation at home and abroad.

GI Profile

Notice Date: December 31, 2009

Producing Area: The administrative areas of 11 counties (cities, districts) including Shizhong District, Wutongqiao District, Shawan District, Jinkouhe District, Emeishan City, Qianwei County, Jingyan County, Jiajiang County, Muchuan County, Ebian Yi Autonomous County, and Mabian Yi Autonomous County of Leshan City, Sichuan Province.

峨眉山茶

Mount Emei Tea

在乐山市 3000 多年的文明发展史中，峨眉山茶及其茶文化占有相当重要的位置，它们同乐山儒、释、道文化组成了绚丽多彩且博大精深的文化大观。峨眉山茶属绿茶类，具有扁平直滑、嫩绿油润、清香高长、鲜醇甘爽的品质特征。其滋味醇厚回甘，富含茶多酚、氨基酸、维生素等多种有益人体健康的成分，在国内外享有盛誉。

地理标志概况

公告日期：2009 年 12 月 31 日

产地范围：四川省乐山市市中区、五通桥区、沙湾区、金口河区、峨眉山市、犍为县、井研县、夹江县、沐川县、峨边彝族自治县、马边彝族自治县 11 个县（市、区）现辖行政区域。

Duobei Tea has been a famous tea in Guizhou Province since long ago and its name was derived from its history as a royal tribute during the reign of Emperor Chongzhen in the Ming Dynasty. Liang Heng, a famous culture scholar, visited Puding County and paid his compliment that "auspicious clouds linger around here because of the treasure deep in the mountains". Exactly, the "treasure" is Duobei Tea.

The color of Duobei Tea is clear and the taste is sweet, with a rich fragrance. Puding County has warm winters and cool summers, with good air, temperature, humidity, and water quality. These unique climate resources and the geographical environment are the key to the quality of Duobei Tea.

GI Profile

Notice Date: February 21, 2013

Producing Area: The administrative areas of 11 townships (towns) including Chengguan Town, Huachu Town, Maguan Town, Baiyan Town, Machang Town, Longchang Township, Maodong Township, Bulang Township, Pingshang Township, Jichangpo Township, and Houchang Township of Puding County, Guizhou Province.

朵贝茶

Duobei Tea

朵贝茶产于普定县，属贵州历史名茶。因明代崇祯年间进贡皇室而闻名。文化大家梁衡在普定县考察时赞曰：『一朵祥云不忍去，只因宝贝在深山』，『宝贝』即朵贝茶。

朵贝茶色清味甘，芳香浓郁。普定县冬无严寒，夏无酷暑，空气、温度、湿度、水质条件良好。得天独厚的气候资源、地理环境是朵贝茶品质形成的关键。

地理标志概况

公告日期：2013 年 2 月 21 日

产地范围：贵州省普定县城关镇、化处镇、马官镇、白岩镇、马场镇、龙场乡、猫洞乡、补郎乡、坪上乡、鸡场坡乡、猴场乡 11 个乡镇现辖行政区域。

Fuding White Tea is a minimally fermented tea. The leaf of its grown plant has plump buds covered with silvery-white hairs. The brewed tea looks crystal and shines in a apricot yellow color, and the flavor of the hairs releases when you take a sip, refreshing, sweet, and mellow. Fuding White Tea is produced by taking the high-quality buds and leaves of tea trees grown in the Taimu Mountains area, and by processing through a special fine process without kneading or frying, which neither destroys enzyme activity nor promotes oxidation, and thus retains the natural nutrients in the tea to the greatest extent.

GI Profile

Notice Date: May 4, 2009

Producing Area: The administrative area of Fuding City, Fujian Province.

福鼎白茶

Fuding White Tea

福鼎白茶属微发酵茶，成品芽头肥壮，满披白毫，如银似雪。其汤色杏黄晶亮，入口毫香显露，鲜爽甘醇。福鼎白茶选用生长于太姥山区的优质芽叶，以不经揉炒的特异精细工艺加工而成，既不破坏酶的活性，又不促进氧化作用，最大程度保留茶叶中的天然营养成分。

地理标志概况

公告日期：2009 年 5 月 4 日

产地范围：福建省福鼎市现辖行政区域。

Wuyi Rock Tea has a long history. Wuyi Rock Tea is a semi-fermented oolong tea, and thus has the fragrance of green tea and the sweet mellowness of black tea, ranking it top in the Chinese oolongs. The leaf of Wuyi Rock Tea has a twisted tip, resembling the head of a dragonfly, in a cyan color while showing an oily brown gloss. Wuyi Rock Tea has an excellent quality, "lively, sweet, refreshing, and fragrant", famous for the "rock" flavor of the rock-like spirit and flower-like fragrance.

GI Profile

Notice Date: March 8, 2002

Producing Area: The administrative area of Mount Wuyi City, Fujian Province.

武夷岩茶

Wuyi Rock Tea

武夷岩茶历史悠久，属半发酵的乌龙茶，具有绿茶之清香，红茶之甘醇，是中国乌龙茶中之极品。武夷岩茶形态叶端扭曲，似蜻蜓头，色泽铁青带褐油润。内质『活、甘、清、香』，素以岩骨花香之『岩韵』著称于世。

地理标志概况

公告日期：2002 年 3 月 8 日

产地范围：福建省武夷山市现辖行政区域。

The history of growing tea in Yingde City can be traced back to the Tang Dynasty. The tea-producing area features a karst landform, the soil there is thick and fertile, with a pH between 4.5 and 5. Yunnan Large Leaf tea trees and Fenghuang Shuixian tea trees are taken as the base, with two or three leaves on each bud as raw materials, as such, Yingde Black Tea is prepared through a refinement process including fading, kneading, leavening, drying, duplicating, and selecting. The processed leaf is compact, has an oily color, delicate and even, covered with golden hairs. The brewed tea has an obvious floral aroma, and tastes mellow and sweet.

GI Profile

Notice Date: December 31, 2006

Producing Area: The four major tea areas of East, Central, Northwest, and Southwest of Yingde City, Guangdong Province, from 112°45′ to 113°55′ east longitude, and from 23° 50′ to 24° 33′ north latitude.

英德红茶

Yingde Black Tea

英德种茶历史悠久，最早可追溯至唐代。英德茶区属喀斯特地貌，土层深厚肥沃，pH值介于4.5—5。茶树以云南大叶与凤凰水仙为基础，选取其一芽二、三叶为原料，经萎凋、揉切、发酵、烘干、复制、精选等工序精制而成。英德红茶外形颗粒紧结重实，色泽油润，细嫩匀整，金毫显露，花香明显，滋味浓厚甜润。

地理标志概况

公告日期：2006年12月31日

产地范围：广东省英德市英东、英中、英西北、英西南四大茶区，东经112°45′至113°55′，北纬23°50′至24°33′。

The leaf of Qiandao Rare Tea is straight like a needle and has a fresh green color; if brewed, the tea looks in a bright green color, smells pleasant, and tastes mellow with a lingering sweetness. The leaf hangs upright in a cup of brewed tea, which shows an excellent ornamental value apart from its value as a drink. The above sensory characteristics of Qiandao Rare Tea are generated from the unique natural environment, variety, and production techniques altogether. Qiandao Rare Tea is processed through spreading fresh leaves, fixing greens, shaping as compact strips, rearranging, finishing, and baking to promote the fragrance.

GI Profile

Producing Area: A total of 16 towns, townships, subdistricts, and 84 villages of Jiande City, Zhejiang Province, in the vast area along the Xin'an River, including Lijia Town, Datong Town, Hangtou Town, Shouchang Town, Genglou Subdistrict, Xin'anjiang Subdistrict, Yangxi Subdistrict, Xiaya Town, Lianhua Town, Yangcunqiao Town, Dayang Town, Meicheng Town, Sandu Town, Qiantan Town, and Qintang Township.

千島银珍

Qiandao Rare Tea

千岛银珍茶外形挺直似针，色泽嫩绿鲜活，汤色嫩绿明亮，香高浓郁，鲜醇回甘，冲泡后，悬垂玉立于杯中，具有极佳的饮用和观赏价值。千岛银珍茶以上感官特征由千岛银珍茶独特的自然环境、独特品种、独特生产工艺等要素共同形成。千岛银珍茶经鲜叶摊放—杀青—紧条定形—复理—整理—足火提香工序加工而成。

地理标志概况

产地范围：浙江省建德市境内李家镇、大同镇、航头镇、寿昌镇、更楼街道、新安江街道、洋溪街道、下涯镇、莲花镇、杨村桥镇、大洋镇、梅城镇、三都镇、乾潭镇、钦堂乡等新安江沿岸广大区域，辖 16 个乡镇、街道，84 个村。

Three Cups of Incense Tea is produced in Taishun County, Wenzhou City, Zhejiang Province. Taishun County has a long history of tea production that dates back to the record in *Taishun County Chronicles* since 1633 AD in Ming Dynasty. Taishun Three Cups of Incense Tea selects the delicate buds and leaves of the tea trees in the tea gardens of Taishun mountain and subjects them to a refining process, which forges a unique product style. The tea leaf has a strip-like shape, thin and tight, with distinct hairs, uniform in size, in a crystal green color, with a tender or chestnut-like fragrance that lasts long; if brewed, the tea tastes fresh and rich, looks in a bright color, and the reconstituted leaf is tender and fresh. Taishun Three Cups of Incense Tea is famous for its "rich fragrance and mellowness that can endure several rounds of brewing".

GI Profile

Producing Area: The territory of Taishun County, Wenzhou City, Zhejiang Province.

泰顺三杯香茶

Taishun Three Cups of Incense Tea

三杯香茶产于浙江省温州市泰顺县。泰顺县有悠久的产茶历史，明代崇祯六年《泰顺县志》即有记载。泰顺三杯香茶系采用泰顺高山茶园中的茶树之细嫩芽叶，精工细作而成，形成了独具特色的产品风格。其外形条索细紧苗秀，毫锋显露，大小匀齐，色泽翠绿；内质嫩香或栗香馥郁持久，滋味鲜爽丰厚，汤色绿艳明亮，叶底嫩绿鲜活，以『香高味醇，经久耐泡，三杯犹存余香』而著称。

地理标志概况

产地范围：浙江省温州市泰顺县境内。

A plant of Macheng Chrysanthemum Tea has a large plump flower with white petals and deep yellow stamens. If brewed, the tea is clear, looks in a greenish golden color, and tastes sweet and mellow. It has three major effects of improving eyesight, protecting the liver, and detoxification. The chrysanthemum can be taken to produce tea, wine, and especially medicine to render significant health care effects. Modern steam cleaning and baking technology is applied to producing Macheng Chrysanthemum Tea, and the chrysanthemums are steam-cleaned and baked the same day as they are picked, without being delayed overnight, and then subjected to careful selection manually to retain the natural essence of each flower.

GI Profile

Producing Area: The northern mountainous area of Macheng City, Hubei Province, a total of 5 towns, wherein Futianhe Town is the major source, and some other planting spots are spread in Huangtugang Town, Chengmagang Town, Sanhekou Town, and Shunheji Town.

麻城福白菊

Macheng Chrysanthemum Tea

麻城福白菊朵大肥厚，花瓣玉白，花蕊深黄，汤液清澈、金黄带绿，味甘醇美，具有明目、护肝、解毒三大功效。菊花可作茶，可酿酒，药用、食用，保健效果明显。麻城福白菊采用现代蒸汽杀青烘烤技术，菊花当天采摘，当天蒸汽杀青烘烤，无隔夜存放，再经人工精心拣选，保证每一朵花自然天成。

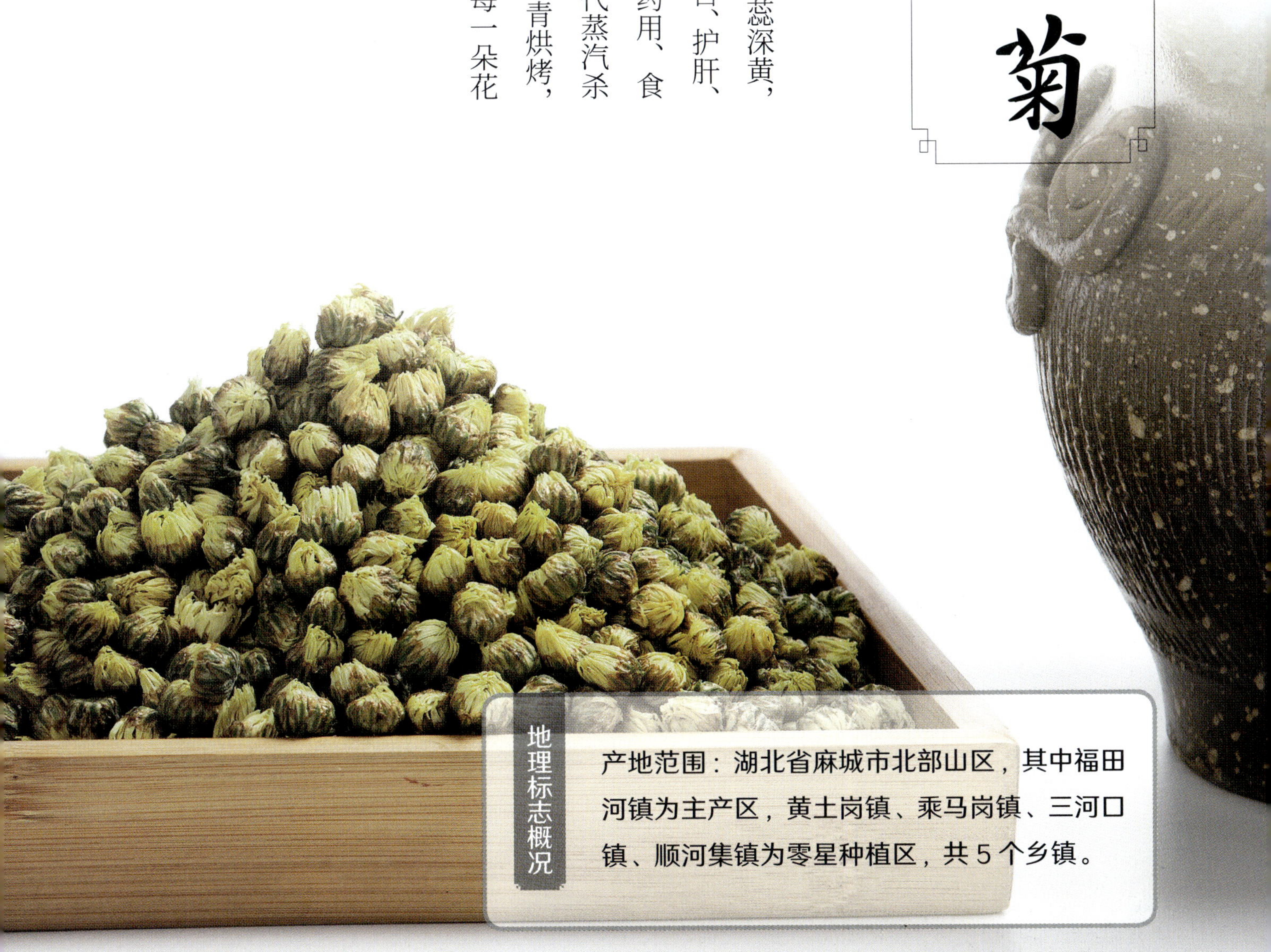

地理标志概况

产地范围：湖北省麻城市北部山区，其中福田河镇为主产区，黄土岗镇、乘马岗镇、三河口镇、顺河集镇为零星种植区，共 5 个乡镇。

Yidu Black Tea is unique in quality and rich in nutrients. For the selected products, the leaf has a strip-like shape, tight and uniform, black and oily with a golden luster, and has a high purity; if brewed, the tea is red and bright, the reconstituted leaves are tender, uniform and red, with strong and long-lasting aroma, and taste fresh and mellow. For the commodities, the leaf has a strip-like shape, black and oily, with good purity; if brewed, the tea looks red and bright, the aroma is pure, the reconstituted leaves are red and uniform, and the taste is mellow.

GI Profile

Producing Area: The entire territory of Yidu City, Hubei Province, including Honghuatao Town, Gaobazhou Town, Yaojiadian Town, Wuyanquan Town, Niejiahe Town, Panjiawan Township of Tujia ethnic people, Wangjiafan Township, Songmuping Town, Zhicheng Town, and Lucheng Subdistrict.

宜都宜红茶

Yidu Black Tea

宜都宜红茶品质独特，内质丰富。名优茶：条索紧细且匀齐，乌黑油润显金毫，净度好；汤色红亮，叶底嫩匀红明，香气浓郁持久，滋味鲜醇。大宗茶：条索紧结且匀整，乌黑油润，净度好；汤色红明，香气纯正，叶底尚红匀，滋味醇和。

地理标志概况

产地范围：湖北省宜都市全境，包括红花套镇、高坝洲镇、姚家店镇、五眼泉镇、聂家河镇、潘家湾土家族乡、王家畈乡、松木坪镇、枝城镇、陆城街道办事处。

The leaves of Guiping Xishan Tea are thin and tender, with distinct hairs, in a shiny greenish blue color; the brewed tea is crystal and clear and tastes unique. Spring tea has a tender aroma, summer tea has a pear flower-like fragrance, autumn tea has a mellow fragrance, and winter tea has a lotus-like fragrance. The tea tastes mellow, sweet after bitterness, and refreshing, with a lingering fragrance in the mouth.

GI Profile

Producing Area: All the administrative townships and towns within the jurisdiction of Guiping City, Guangxi Zhuang Autonomous Region, namely Xishan Town, Mengxu Town, Shilong Town, Houlu Township, Baisha Town, Nanmu Town, Jintian Town, Dongxin Township, Zijing Town, Jiangkou Town, Mule Town , Mugui Town, Shizui Town, Mapi Township, Youma Town, Shepo Town, Xunwang Township, Luoxiu Town, Zhongsha Town, Dayang Town, Luobo Township, Mugen Town, Madong Town, Shebu Town, Xiawan Town, and Dawan Town, covering 26 townships (towns), 414 administrative villages, 7,763 villager groups, and 1 state-owned forest farm.

桂平西山茶

Guiping Xishan Tea

桂平西山茶叶嫩条细，苗锋显露，色质青黛而呈光泽，汤液碧绿而清澈透亮。其茶味独具特色，春茶清香，夏茶梨香，秋茶醇香，冬茶莲香，滋味醇和，回甘鲜爽，饮后齿颊留香。

地理标志概况

产地范围：广西壮族自治区桂平市辖区内所有行政乡镇，即西山镇、蒙圩镇、石龙镇、厚禄乡、白沙镇、南木镇、金田镇、垌心乡、紫荆镇、江口镇、木乐镇、木圭镇、石咀镇、马皮乡、油麻镇、社坡镇、寻旺乡、罗秀镇、中沙镇、大洋镇、罗播乡、木根镇、麻垌镇、社步镇、下湾镇、大湾镇26个乡镇，414个行政村、7763个村民小组、1个国有林场。

Naxi District has a long history of tea production and is known as a region where tea trees germinate first at the same latitude in the world because of its unique geographical and climatic conditions. Fresh tea can be harvested in early February of each year and put on sale as early as New Year's Eve, therefore, the tea is also named "New Year's Eve Tea". Naxi Early-Spring Tea is characterized by "early harvest, excellent quality, and fragrance", the product leaves have a flat and straight shape, a uniform length, clean and smooth, in a crystal green color, with a chestnut-like aroma; the brewed tea has a fresh fragrance, looks in a bright yellow-green color, tastes mellow and refreshing. The reconstituted leaves are complete, tender and uniform, in a yellowish green color.

GI Profile

Producing Area: A total of 176 villages in 12 towns of Naxi District, Luzhou City, Sichuan Province, including Dadukou, Huguo, Dagu, Shangma, Hemian, Fengle, Baijie, Tianxian, Mianhuapo, Xinle, Quba, and Longche. This area borders Hejiang County in the east, Xuyong County in the south, Jiang'an County in the west, and Jiangyang District, Luzhou City in the north.

纳溪特早茶

Naxi Early-Spring Tea

纳溪区产茶历史久远，因其独特的地理气候条件，是全球同纬度茶树萌发最早的区域，常年二月初就可以采制新茶，最早在除夕便能尝到新茶，有『除夕茶』的美誉。纳溪特早茶以『早、优、香』为主要特点，产品外形扁平挺直，长短匀整，洁净光滑，色泽翠绿，香气栗香带清香，汤色黄绿明亮，滋味鲜醇爽口，叶底完整，嫩匀黄绿。

地理标志概况

产地范围：四川省泸州市纳溪区的大渡口、护国、打古、上马、合面、丰乐、白节、天仙、棉花坡、新乐、渠坝、龙车 12 个镇的 176 个村，东连合江县，南接叙永县，西界江安县，北邻泸州市江阳区。

Baoshan City, one of the three major producing areas of Arabica coffee in Yunnan, has a long history of cultivating Arabica coffee, which can date back to the mid-1950s, and knowledge and experience have accumulated since then. The unique dry-warm valley climate in the Lujiang Dam area of Baoshan City contributes to the unique flavor and characteristics of the coffee. Baoshan Arabica Coffee tastes mellow without bitterness, smells in faint fragrance, tender and pleasant. It contains rich oil and strong fruit acid, featuring lingering sweetness, which brings a fresh and pleasant experience and unforgettable wonderful feelings when you drink.

GI Profile

Notice Date: December 24, 2010

Producing Area: The administrative areas of 5 counties and districts including Longyang District, Longling County, Shidian County, Changning County, and Tengchong County of Baoshan City, Yunnan Province.

保山小粒咖啡

Baoshan Arabica Coffee

作为云南小粒咖啡三大产区之一的保山产区，小粒咖啡种植历史悠久，栽培经验丰富，可追溯到 20 世纪 50 年代中期。保山潞江坝独特的干热河谷气候条件造就了保山小粒咖啡独特的风味特征。保山小粒咖啡具有浓而不苦、香而不烈、香味醇和、含油丰富、果酸浓厚、回甘持久的特点，带给饮用者清新淡雅的香味体验和入口难忘的美妙感受。

地理标志概况

公告日期：2010 年 12 月 24 日

产地范围：云南省保山市隆阳区、龙陵县、施甸县、昌宁县、腾冲县 5 个县区现辖行政区域。

Xinglong Coffee is produced in Xinglong Town, Wanning City, Hainan Province, which is located at 18.8 degrees north latitude, the best location in the "coffee belt", having soil rich in selenium. The special geographical environment and climate contribute to the significantly higher caffeine content in coffee beans in Xinglong than elsewhere. Generations of coffeemakers have refined and improved on the basis of the conventional roasting technique in Southeast Asia, and forged a unique roasting technique for Xinglong Coffee. As such, Xinglong Coffee has a unique flavor of "tender fragrance and mellowness without bitterness", and is highly recognized in the market.

GI Profile

Notice Date: December 26, 2007

Producing Area: The administrative areas including Xinglong Overseas Chinese Farm, Nanqiao Town, Changfeng Town, Niulouxu, Sangengluo Town, and Liji Town of Wanning City, Hainan Province.

兴隆咖啡

Xinglong Coffee

兴隆咖啡产于海南省万宁市兴隆镇。地处北纬18.8度『咖啡带』黄金地带，兴隆土壤内含硒丰富，特殊的地理环境、气候条件，使得兴隆咖啡豆中的咖啡因含量明显高于其他地区。经历了几代咖啡人不断的锤炼和提高，兴隆咖啡在东南亚传统焙炒工艺的基础上形成了独特的焙炒技术。兴隆咖啡『香而不烈，浓而不苦』的独特风味备受市场认可。

地理标志概况

公告日期：2007 年 12 月 26 日

产地范围：海南省万宁市兴隆华侨农场、南桥镇、长丰镇、牛漏墟、三更罗镇、礼纪镇现辖行政区域。

The stem of the plant is straight with nodes; each node has a pair of leaves in a green color; the flowers are white, androgynous, and usually bloom from March to April; the ripe fruits are round red or yellow berries, after peeling, a fresh fruit usually contains two seeds, and the fresh fruit becomes generally ripe from October to February next year. Pu'er Coffee has a pleasant color and high quality, characterized by "strong flavor without bitterness, tender fragrance, and slight sour taste", recognized as a first-class product by the International Coffee Organization (ICO).

GI Profile

Producing Area: The administrative area under the jurisdiction of Pu'er City, Yunnan Province.

普洱咖啡

Pu'er Coffee

普洱咖啡茎为直生，茎上有节；每个节上有1对叶片，绿色；花为白色，雌雄同花，盛花期一般在三月至四月；成熟鲜果为圆形红色（黄色）浆果，鲜果脱皮后一般多为2粒籽，鲜果成熟期一般在十月至次年二月。普洱咖啡色泽好、品质优，具有『浓而不苦、香而不烈、略带果酸味』的独特品质特征，被国际咖啡组织（ICO）认定为一类产品。

地理标志概况

产地范围：云南省普洱市现辖行政区域。

Wuchuan Mooncake dates back to the Southern Song Dynasty. Up till now, it has become a token of a happy reunion. Wuchuan Mooncake is characterized by being large in size, thin in crust, rich in fillings, and fragrant in smell. Its contour is mainly a round cake. Its dominating raw materials include shelled melon seeds, sesame kernels, walnut kernels, almonds, olive kernels, pork, hams and the like. The baked mooncakes have full individuals, an oily, smooth and brownish yellow color, a thin and soft crust, rich fillings, a fragrant and sweet taste, and a lasting aftertaste, representing a rich local flavor and custom features.

GI Profile

Notice Date: June 26, 2013

Producing Area: The administrative area of Wuchuan City, Guangdong Province.

吴川月饼

Wuchuan Mooncake

吴川月饼起源于南宋，至今已成为寄托团圆美满的象征。吴川月饼的特点是个大、皮薄、馅多、味香，外形以圆形大饼为主，主要原料为瓜子仁、芝麻仁、核桃仁、杏仁、橄榄仁、猪肉、火腿等，烘焙后的月饼个体饱满，色泽油润棕黄，饼皮薄且松软，馅料丰富，味道香甜，食后颊齿留香，具有浓厚的地方韵味和风俗特色。

地理标志概况

公告日期：2013 年 6 月 26 日

产地范围：广东省吴川市现辖行政区。

味鲜美，咸淡适口，质地脆嫩，菜段均匀。

榨菜：具有特有的鲜香味及其辅料滋味，可配制各种味型，质地脆嫩。

大头菜：深褐色，有光泽，发酵香气浓郁，味鲜，咸淡适口，组织致密，质地脆嫩，菜形均匀。

Pickled vegetables: glossy with strong aroma from well-prepared pickling, neither too salty nor too sour (sweet), with refreshing fragrance, tender and crispy in nature, and uniform in shape and size, and the pickling water is clear. Seasoned pickles: glossy with strong aroma from salting pickling, neither too salty nor too sour (sweet) nor too spicy, with refreshing taste, tender and crispy in nature, and uniform in shape and size. Chili-made broad-bean sauce: bright reddish brown with rich sauce or spicy flavor, fresh and strong in aroma, with endless aftertastes, neither too thin nor thick, with chili pieces or broad beans and other auxiliary materials in a vision of your naked eyes. Pickled bean sprouts: bright brown yellow, with strong fermentation aroma, fragrant, favorably tasty with sweet aftertastes, tender and crispy in nature, and uniform in shape and size. Preserved cabbage (also called Dong Cai Jian): bright brown or dark brown, with strong fermentation aroma, fragrant, with favorable sweet aftertastes, tender and crispy in nature, and uniform in shape and size. Preserved szechuan pickles: unique in fresh flavor with taste of its auxiliaries, varies in flavors and tender and crispy in nature. Turnips: bright dark brown, with strong fermentation aroma and refreshing flavor, favorably tasty with sweet aftertastes, tender and crispy in nature, and uniform in shape and size.

GI Profile

Producing Area: Chengdu City, Zigong City, Panzhihua City, Luzhou City, Deyang City, Neijiang City, Leshan City, Mianyang City, Suining City, Guangyuan City, Nanchong City, Yibin City, Guang'an City, Dazhou City, Meishan City, Ziyang City, Bazhong City, Ya'an City, Aba Prefecture, Ganzi Prefecture, Liangshan Prefecture under jurisdiction of Sichuan Province.

四川泡菜

Sichuan Style Pickles

泡渍泡菜：有光泽，泡渍发酵香气浓郁，咸酸（甜）适宜，清香爽口，质地脆嫩，菜形大小均匀，汤汁清亮。

调味泡菜：有光泽，盐渍调味香气浓郁，咸酸（甜）适宜或麻辣适度，鲜香可口，质地脆嫩，菜形大小均匀。

辣椒豆瓣：色泽红褐色，油润有光泽，酱酯香或辣香浓郁，味鲜辣醇厚，回味悠长，黏稠适度，可见辣椒块或蚕豆瓣粒及其他辅料。

芽菜：色泽褐黄，润泽发亮，发酵香气浓郁，气味甜香，咸淡适口，回味甘甜，质地脆嫩，菜段均匀。

冬菜（尖）：色泽褐色或乌褐色，有光泽，发酵香气浓郁，

地理标志概况

产地范围：四川省辖区内的成都市、自贡市、攀枝花市、泸州市、德阳市、内江市、乐山市、绵阳市、遂宁市、广元市、南充市、宜宾市、广安市、达州市、眉山市、资阳市、巴中市、雅安市、阿坝州、甘孜州和凉山州21个市（州）。

Yibin Bean Sprout selects high-quality Erpingzhuang as raw materials. By adhering to the traditional fermentation process, Yibin Bean Sprout has gradually formed its own unique flavor, and has passed down from generation to generation to become a well-known brand of traditional pickled vegetable in Southwest China.

Pits are necessary facilities for the fermentation of Yibin Bean Sprout and they have witnessed the continuation of the ancient pickling method of Yibin Bean Sprout as well as the unremitting innovation and transformation of diced Yibin Bean Sprout. Pits where diced Yibin Bean Sprout traditionally ferments allow Bean Sprout to ferment three times in different pits successively to form a unique flavor of "fragrant, sweet, crispy, tender and fresh".

GI Profile

Notice Date: February 12, 2004

Producing Area: The administrative area of Yibin City, Sichuan Province.

宜宾芽菜

Yibin Bean Sprout

宜宾芽菜严选优质二平桩为原料，坚持传统发酵工艺，逐渐形成了自己独特的风味，并代代相传，成为中国西南地区家喻户晓的传统酱腌菜品牌。

窖池是宜宾芽菜发酵的必要设施，它们见证了宜宾芽菜古法腌制的延续，也见证着宜宾芽菜不断的创新与改造。窖池，宜宾芽菜传统发酵的地方，让芽菜先后在不同的池中经过三次发酵，形成『香、甜、脆、嫩、鲜』的独特风味。

地理标志概况

公告日期：2004 年 2 月 12 日

产地范围：四川省宜宾市现辖行政区域。

Dating back to the years of Datong in the Southern Liang Dynasty, Turpan Raisin has a long history. Turpan has a hot and dry climate. Turpan Raisins, made by natural air drying, have pure color, full grain, soft pulp, palatable flavor, mildly sweet and sour taste. Moreover, they are rich in natural fructose, protein, vitamins, cellulose and many trace elements required by the human body, being a multi-purpose pure natural healthy food.

GI Profile

Notice Date: June 25, 2003

Producing Area: The administrative area of Turpan City (Gaochang District, Shanshan County, and Tuokexun County), Xinjiang Uygur Autonomous Region.

吐鲁番葡萄干

Turpan Raisin

吐鲁番葡萄干历史悠久，可追溯至南朝梁国大同年间。吐鲁番气候炎热而干燥，自然风干的吐鲁番葡萄干色泽纯正，果粒饱满，肉质细软，味道鲜美，酸甜适口，并含有丰富的天然果糖、蛋白质、维生素、纤维素以及人体所需的多种微量元素，是一种多用途纯天然健康食品。

地理标志概况

公告日期：2003 年 6 月 25 日

产地范围: 新疆维吾尔自治区吐鲁番市（高昌区、鄯善县和托克逊县）现辖行政区域。

It is said that, in the late Ming Dynasty and early Qing Dynasty, immigrants into Sichuan Province began to produce Pixian Bean Paste. During the reign of Emperor Kangxi in Qing Dynasty (1688 AD), the descendants inherited the production method of Pixian Bean Paste. They took local raw materials and clean water to produce Bean Paste in large quantities by this method. Since then, this condiment has been known as "Pixian Bean Paste".

Under the special climate, soil, water quality and other geographical environment, Pixian Bean Paste is prepared by selecting premium red peppers, second-rate green broad beans, high-quality flour, and refined edible salt, which are mixed in a vat after salting, starter-making, and fermenting, and treated with natural brewing and fermenting through traditional processes such as long-term turning, drying in the sun, and outdoor exposure. Pixian Bean Paste has the characteristics of crispy petals, rich sauce, reddish brown color, lasting and mellow aftertaste and being oily and shiny, spicy but not dry, and moderately viscous. It is known as "the soul of Sichuan cuisine".

GI Profile

Notice Date: December 31, 2005

Producing Area: The administrative area of Pixian County, Chengdu City, Sichuan Province.

郫县豆瓣

Pixian Bean Paste

相传明末清初，入蜀移民便开始了郫县豆瓣的生产。清康熙年间（公元 1688 年），后人传承此道，取当地原料与清水，以此法大量生产豆瓣，『郫县豆瓣』亦始得名。

郫县豆瓣精选上等红辣椒，二流瓣青皮蚕豆、优质面粉、精制食用盐，在特殊的气候、土壤、水质等地理环境下，经过盐渍、制曲、发酵拌和入缸，通过长期翻、晒、露等传统工艺天然精酿发酵而成，具有瓣子酥脆化渣、酱脂香浓郁、红褐油润有光泽、辣而不燥、黏稠适度、回味醇厚悠长的特点，有『川菜之魂』之称。

地理标志概况

公告日期：2005 年 12 月 31 日

产地范围：四川省成都市郫县现辖行政区域。

Shanxi Aged Vinegar is produced in Taiyuan City and Jinzhong City, Shanxi Province, where the temperature and humidity are suitable for the reproduction of the microbial system required for vinegar brewing. The brewing process of Shanxi Aged Vinegar is summarized as five major steps of "steaming, fermenting, smoking, leaching and aging". This set of techniques is unique among Chinese vinegar brewing technologies, and is a typical representative of the inheritance and continuous development of traditional Chinese techniques, becoming a shining pearl in China's intangible cultural heritage.

GI Profile

Notice Date: August 9, 2004

Producing Area: The administrative areas of Qingxu County, Xinghualing District, Wanbolin District, Xiaodian District, Yingze District, Jinyuan District, and Jiancaoping District of Taiyuan City, and Yuci District, Taigu County, and Qixian County of Jinzhong City, Shanxi Province.

山西老陈醋

Shanxi Aged Vinegar

山西老陈醋产自山西省太原市和晋中市，该地的温度与湿度适合酿醋所需微生物体系的繁殖。山西老陈醋的酿造工艺被概括为『蒸、酵、熏、淋、陈』五大步。这套技艺在中国酿醋技术上独树一帜，是中国传统技艺传承并不断发展的一个典型代表，是中国非物质文化遗产中的一颗璀璨明珠。

地理标志概况

公告日期：2004 年 8 月 9 日

产地范围：山西省太原市的清徐县、杏花岭区、万柏林区、小店区、迎泽区、晋源区、尖草坪区以及晋中市的榆次区、太谷县、祁县现辖行政区域。

Located in the southwest of Heilongjiang Province, at the hinterland of the Songnen Plain, and in the golden rice production zone at 45 degrees north latitude, Zhaoyuan County is known as the "Jiangnan (known as a rich land in south China) in far north China, and hometown of fish and rice". Chernozem with local characteristics, which is fertile in soil quality, high in organic matter content, and high in water holding capacity, provides a good and healthy development environment for the growth of rice, creating high-quality "Zhaoyuan Rice". Zhaoyuan Rice is long-grained with full grains, white like pearls and jades, crystal clear, and rich in fresh fragrance. The cooked rice is white, smooth, tough and chewy, and satiny, and has a mellow flavor and excellent taste.

GI Profile

Notice Date: June 2, 2009

Producing Area: The administrative area of Zhaoyuan County, Heilongjiang Province.

肇源大米

Zhaoyuan Rice

肇源县地处黑龙江省西南部，松嫩平原腹地，北纬45度黄金水稻生产带上，素有『塞北江南、鱼米之乡』的美誉。此地特有的黑钙土土质肥沃，有机质含量高，蓄水能力强，为水稻生长提供了良好的健康发育环境，孕育出品质优良的『肇源大米』。肇源大米呈长粒型，粒饱满、如珠似玉、晶莹剔透、清香浓郁，做出的米饭洁白光润、品味香醇、筋道滑腻、口感极佳。

地理标志概况

公告日期：2009年6月2日

产地范围：黑龙江省肇源县现辖行政区域。

Wuchang, the "hometown of high-quality rice" in China, is in the southern part of Heilongjiang Province. Wuchang Rice has a long planting history and unique taste quality. Its characteristics are generalized as "crystal clear appearance, good taste; soft, glutinous, fragrant and sweet flavor; and the feature that it doesn't harden after cooling", winning great favor from the consumers. Nowadays, Wuchang is committed to making Wuchang Rice the world's top rice brand in accordance with the protection working concepts of good environment, good water quality, good soil, good climate, and good variety.

GI Profile

Notice Date: May 10, 2003

Producing Area: The administrative area of Wuchang City, Heilongjiang Province.

五常大米

Wuchang Rice

五常市是中国的『优质稻米之乡』，位于黑龙江省南部，大米种植历史悠久。五常大米口感品质独特，其特点可以概括为『晶莹剔透，口感佳；软糯香甜，不回生』，备受消费者青睐。如今，五常市按照『环境好、水质好、土壤好、气候好、品种好』的保护工作思路，致力于将五常大米品牌打造成世界顶级稻米品牌。

地理标志概况

公告日期：2003 年 5 月 10 日

产地范围：黑龙江省五常市现辖行政区域。

Originating from 1894, rice cultivation in Panjin City has a long history. Panjin City is located in the golden area for high-quality rice, which makes Panjin Rice featured with low amylose content, and high gel consistency. Panjin Rice has a bluish white and shiny appearance, oval grain, full and complete grain shape, high rice grain strength, and few broken pieces; the steamed and boiled rice is oily in color, fragrant, soft, chewy and smooth, and sweet in taste, and after cooling, Panjin Rice does not harden and still maintains a soft and moist flavor.

GI Profile

Notice Date: September 10, 2002

Producing Area: The administrative area of Panjin City, Liaoning Province.

盘锦大米

Panjin Rice

盘锦市的水稻种植源于1894年，历史悠久。盘锦市位于优质黄金稻区，造就了盘锦大米直链淀粉含量低、胶稠度高等特性。盘锦大米外观青白而有光泽，籽粒呈椭圆形，粒形饱满完整，米粒强度高、破碎少；蒸煮后的米饭色泽油润，吃起来香软弹滑，有甜味，冷却后不回生，仍能保持软润的口感。

地理标志概况

公告日期：2002 年 9 月 10 日

产地范围：辽宁省盘锦市现辖行政区域。

Rice is a reputational iconic crop in the Yellow River Irrigation District in Ningxia, known as "Saishangjiangnan" (an abundant place beyond the frontier as the southern regions of the Yangtze River), with a long history of rice cultivation and superior natural conditions. Due to the dry climate, sufficient sunshine, large temperature difference between day and night, light diseases and insect pests, few pollution sources, the rice produced has a smooth, crystal clear, delicate and shiny surface, and a sticky but not greasy, smooth, refreshing, excellent taste. Ningxia Rice is high in protein, rich in a variety of vitamins and trace elements.

GI Profile

Producing Area: The alluvial plain of the Yellow River (called Ningxia Plain) in north-central of Ningxia Hui Autonomous Region.

宁夏大米

Ningxia Rice

大米是宁夏引黄灌区『塞上江南』美誉的标志性作物，该区域种植大米历史悠久，自然条件优越，气候干燥，日照充足，昼夜温差大，病虫害轻，污染源少，生产的大米表面光滑，晶莹剔透，细腻油亮，入口黏而不腻，滑润爽口，口感极佳。宁夏大米蛋白质含量高，富含多种维生素和微量元素。

地理标志概况

产地范围：宁夏回族自治区中北部的黄河冲积平原（称宁夏平原）。

Baicheng Mung Bean is produced in Baicheng City, Jilin Province. Baicheng City belongs to a semi-arid agricultural ecological zone with sufficient sunlight and abundant heat resources. Therefore, Baicheng Mung Bean has distinct features of large grain, full shape, bright color, emerald green, no mixed color, no pollution, high protein content and the like. Compared with mung beans produced in other producing areas, Baicheng Mung Bean has good glossiness, neat grain shape and no peculiar smell.

GI Profile

Notice Date: April 23, 2007

Producing Area: The administrative area of Baicheng City, Jilin Province.

白城绿豆

Baicheng Mung Bean

白城绿豆产于吉林省白城市。白城市属于半干旱农业生态区，光照充足、热量资源丰富。在此气候条件下生长出的白城绿豆有颗粒大、形状饱满、色泽明亮、颜色鲜绿、无杂色、无污染、含蛋白质高等明显特点。与其他产区绿豆相比，白城绿豆光泽度好、粒形整齐、无异味。

地理标志概况

公告日期：2007 年 4 月 23 日

产地范围：吉林省白城市现辖行政区域。

The growth period of spring-sown open-field cultivation of Hengshan Daming Mung Bean is 105-115 days. It has an erect plant type, broadly ovoid leaves in dark green, and yellow-green flowers, with an indeterminate podding habit. Pods are black when they are mature, and grains are cylindrical, dark green and shiny. Raw bean sprouts are white in color, tender in texture, and sweet and crispy in taste. The produced bean sprouts grow neatly, and are uniform in thickness and resistant to high temperatures. They can be produced and sold throughout the year.

GI Profile

Producing Area: Within Hengshan County, Yulin City, Shaanxi Province, the planting area is bordered by Yuyang District in the north, Zizhou County and Zichang County in the south, Jingbian County in the west, Mizhi County in the east, and Wushen Banner in Inner Mongolia in the northwest. The planting administrative region belongs to 358 administrative villages in 18 townships, including Dangcha, Wuzhen Town, Gaozhen Town, Shiyaogou, Hancha, Dianshi, Nanta, Xiangshui, Boluo, Baijie, Leilongwan, Hengshan Town, Zhaoshipan, Tawan, Aihaomao, Shuangcheng, Shiwan, and Weijialou, as well as 10 branching fields of Shimagua Farm in Hengshan County, Shaanxi Province.

横山大明绿豆

Hengshan Daming Mung Bean

横山大明绿豆春播露地栽培生育期为105—115天，其株型直立，叶片阔卵圆形，叶色浓绿，花为黄绿色，具有无限结荚习性，豆荚成熟时呈黑色，籽粒呈圆柱形，深绿色有光泽。生产的豆芽色白、质嫩、口感甜脆；生长整齐、粗细均匀、耐高温，一年四季均可生产销售。

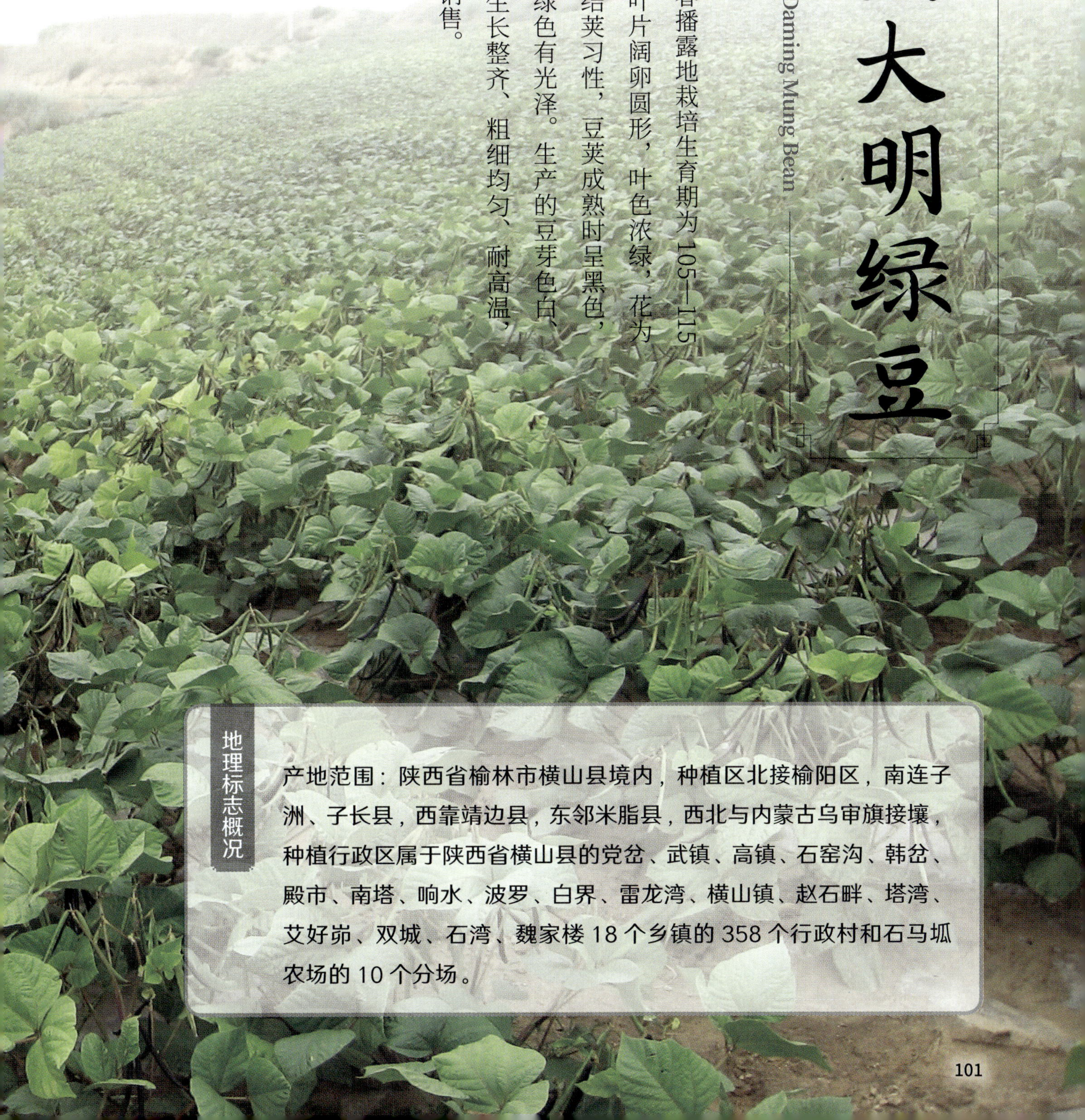

地理标志概况

产地范围：陕西省榆林市横山县境内，种植区北接榆阳区，南连子洲、子长县，西靠靖边县，东邻米脂县，西北与内蒙古乌审旗接壤，种植行政区属于陕西省横山县的党岔、武镇、高镇、石窑沟、韩岔、殿市、南塔、响水、波罗、白界、雷龙湾、横山镇、赵石畔、塔湾、艾好峁、双城、石湾、魏家楼18个乡镇的358个行政村和石马坬农场的10个分场。

Gannan is a well-known navel orange production base in China, known as the "Hometown of Navel Oranges in China". A large number of shallow hills and slopes, red loam with deep soil layers, and warm and humid climate have created unique conditions for the development of high-quality navel orange orchards. Gannan Navel Orange has large fruit, thin peel, bright orange-red color, good-looking appearance, crisp and tender flesh, fragrance and refreshing taste, rich nutrition and high quality.

GI Profile

Notice Date: September 27, 2004

Producing Area: The administrative areas of 18 counties (cities, districts) and 1 National Development Zone including Xinfeng County, Xunwu County, Anyuan County, Ganxian County, Nankang District, Yudu County, Dingnan County, Longnan County, Ruijin City, Huichang County, Xingguo County, Zhanggong District, Ningdu County, Dayu County, Quannan County, Chongyi County (excluding Shangbao Township and Ledong Township), Shangyou County (excluding Anhe Township, Sixia Township, Shuangxi Township, Shuiyan Township, Pingfu Township, Wuzhifeng Township, and Doushui Town), Shicheng County (excluding Gaotian Town and Mulan Township), and Ganzhou Economic and Technological Development Zone of Ganzhou City, Jiangxi Province.

赣南脐橙

Gannan Navel Orange

赣南为我国著名的脐橙生产基地，被称为『中国脐橙之乡』。大量的浅丘坡地，土层深厚的红壤土及温暖湿润的气候，为发展高品质脐橙果园创造了得天独厚的条件。赣南脐橙果大皮薄、橙红鲜艳、外形美观、肉质脆嫩、清香爽口、营养丰富、品质上乘。

地理标志概况

公告日期：2004 年 9 月 27 日

产地范围：江西省赣州市所辖信丰县、寻乌县、安远县、赣县、南康区、于都县、定南县、龙南县、瑞金市、会昌县、兴国县、章贡区、宁都县、大余县、全南县、崇义县（不包括上堡乡、乐洞乡）、上犹县（不包括安和乡、寺下乡、双溪乡、水岩乡、平富乡、五指峰乡、陡水镇）、石城县（不包括高田镇、木兰乡）、赣州经济技术开发区 18 个县（市、区）和 1 个国家级开发区现辖行政区域。

In 1871, a new era of Western apple cultivation was inaugurated in Yantai City, China. Surrounded by sea on three sides, Yantai has a hilly topography, with soil rich in minerals, and moderate temperature difference between day and night, which creates the unique quality of Yantai Apple. Yantai Apple is well-known at home and abroad for its "regular shape, bright color, sweet and crisp pulp, and strong aroma". It is exported to more than 60 countries and regions including the Southeast Asia, the United States, and the European Union.

GI Profile

Notice Date: August 28, 2002

Producing Area: The administrative area of Yantai City, Shandong Province.

烟台苹果

Yantai Apple

1871 年，烟台市开创了中国西洋苹果栽培的新纪元。三面环海，丘陵地貌，土壤富含矿物质，昼夜温差适中，造就了烟台苹果独特的品质。烟台苹果以『果形端正、色泽艳丽、果肉甜脆、香气浓郁』享誉国内外。烟台苹果出口东南亚、美国、欧盟等 60 多个国家和地区。

地理标志概况

公告日期：2002 年 8 月 28 日

产地范围：山东省烟台市现辖行政区域。

Nanfeng Sweet Orange is produced in Nanfeng County, Fuzhou City, Jiangxi Province, with a cultivation history of more than 1,300 years. Since the Tang Dynasty, it has been listed as a tribute by successive imperial families. Moistened by the subtropical monsoon climate, coupled with the cultivation of red loam and paddy soil of the hilly and mountainous regions in the southeast of Jiangxi, Nanfeng Sweet Orange has excellent qualities such as "oblate shape, golden color, thin peel and juicy pulp, mildly sour and sweet taste, few seeds and residues inside, distinctive flavor, and rich nutrition". It is well received by the market.

GI Profile

Notice Date: February 12, 2003

Producing Area: The administrative area of Nanfeng County, Jiangxi Province.

南丰蜜桔

Nanfeng Sweet Orange

南丰蜜桔产于江西省抚州市南丰县，距今已有1300多年的栽培历史，自唐代以来，被历代皇室列为贡品。受亚热带季风气候的滋润，加之赣东南丘陵山地红壤土和水稻土的培育，南丰蜜桔具有『圆润秀小、色泽金黄、皮薄多汁、酸甜适口、少核化渣、清香独特、营养丰富』的优良品质，深受市场认可。

地理标志概况

公告日期：2003年2月12日

产地范围：江西省南丰县现辖行政区域。

Korla Pear grows in Korla City, Xinjiang Uygur Autonomous Region, where the soil is fertile and the light and heat resources are excellent. Its fruit has a cylindrical, regular, smooth, attractive and beautiful appearance, as well as the characteristics such as strong aroma, thin skin, tender flesh, crispy and refreshing taste, rich juice and few residues, bright and pleasant green color, and storage resistance, and contains rich glucose, Alpha hydroxyl acid, iron, vitamins and other trace elements. Korla Pear, with high nutritional value, is dubbed as the "Queen of Pears in the World".

GI Profile

Notice Date: December 31, 2004

Producing Area: The administrative areas of 3 cities and 7 counties including Korla City, Yuli County, Luntai County, Aksu City, Alaer City, Kuqa County, Shaya County, Xinhe County, Awat County, and Wensu County of Xinjiang Uygur Autonomous Region.

库尔勒香梨

Korla Pear

库尔勒香梨生长在土质肥沃、光热资源良好的新疆维吾尔自治区库尔勒市，其果实呈圆柱形、端正、整齐、美观，外形漂亮，具有香气浓郁、皮薄肉细、酥脆爽口、汁多渣少、色泽翠绿悦目、耐贮藏等特性；富含葡萄糖、果酸、铁、维生素等成分，营养价值很高，被誉为『世界梨后』。

地理标志概况

公告日期：2004 年 12 月 31 日

产地范围：新疆维吾尔自治区的库尔勒市、尉犁县、轮台县、阿克苏市、阿拉尔市、库车县、沙雅县、新和县、阿瓦提县、温宿县 3 市 7 县现辖行政区域。

Anyue Lemon has a history dating back to 1929. Hailed as the "City of Lemons in China" for over 90 years, Anyue County, Sichuan Province, is China's lemon commodity production base county and also one of the world's five largest lemon producing areas. Thanks to the unique local natural conditions and years of experience in cultivation and domestication, Anyue Lemon has a high yield, good quality, good taste, and high nutritional value.

GI Profile

Notice Date: January 14, 2007

Producing Area: The administrative area of Anyue County, Sichuan Province.

安岳柠檬

Anyue Lemon

安岳柠檬的历史可以追溯到 1929 年，90 多年来，四川省安岳县素有『中国柠檬之都』的美称，是中国的柠檬商品生产基地县，也是世界五大柠檬产区之一。得益于当地得天独厚的自然条件，以及多年的栽培驯化经验，安岳柠檬产量高、品质好、味道佳、营养价值高。

地理标志概况

公告日期：2007 年 1 月 14 日

产地范围：四川省安岳县现辖行政区域。

Starting in the 1980s, Jingning Apple, produced in Jingning County, Gansu Province, is regular in shape, high in pile, bright in color, smooth in surface, free of pollution, fine in pulp, juicy, mildly sweet and sour, and resistant to storage and transportation. With unique geographical conditions and advanced planting experience, Jingning County is known worldwide as the "Hometown of Apples in China", and also enjoys the reputation of "preferring Jingning Apple to any other apples all over the world".

GI Profile

Notice Date: September 4, 2006

Producing Area: 20 townships (towns) including Renda Township, Lidian Town, Zhiping Township, Shengou Township, Jiahe Township, Yuwan Township, Leida Township, Shuangxian Township, Gangou Township, Xindian Township, Gucheng Township, Chengguan Town, Chengchuan Township, Weirong Town, Siqiao Township, Sihe Township, Hongsi Township, Xixiang Township, Jieshipu Town, and Bali Town of Jingning County, Gansu Province.

静宁苹果

Jingning Apple

甘肃省静宁县所产的静宁苹果起步于 20 世纪 80 年代，果形端正，高桩，色泽鲜艳，果面光洁，无污染，肉质细，果汁多，酸甜可口，耐贮藏，易运输。

静宁县拥有得天独厚的地理条件，以及先进的种植经验，以『中国苹果之乡』闻名于世，更是享有『吃遍天下苹果，还想静宁苹果』的美誉。

地理标志概况

公告日期：2006 年 9 月 4 日

产地范围：甘肃省静宁县的仁大乡、李店镇、治平乡、深沟乡、贾河乡、余湾乡、雷大乡、双岘乡、甘沟乡、新店乡、古城乡、城关镇、城川乡、威戎镇、司桥乡、四河乡、红寺乡、细巷乡、界石铺镇、八里镇 20 个乡镇。

Cangxi Red Kiwi Fruit, which originated in Cangxi County, Sichuan Province, has a good-looking appearance, and a fruit core with radial red stripes, like the rising sun. The fruit is strong sweet with slight sourness and a thick fragrance, like wild bee honey. It has excellent taste, high quality and lingering aftertaste. It is rich in minerals, vitamins, and anthocyanins. Being superior in quality and unique in characteristics, Cangxi Red Kiwi Fruit is very popular with consumers.

GI Profile

Notice Date: November 21, 2010

Producing Area: All the townships (towns) of Cangxi County, Sichuan Province.

苍溪红心猕猴桃

Cangxi Red Kiwi Fruit

四川省苍溪县是红心猕猴桃的起源地。苍溪红心猕猴桃外形美观，果心呈放射状红色条纹，宛如东升旭日。果实味微酸浓甜，伴有浓浓的馥香，如野生蜂糖，口感极佳，品质上乘，回味悠长。

苍溪红心猕猴桃富含丰富的矿物质、维生素和花青素，果品品质优良，性状独特，深受广大消费者的喜爱。

地理标志概况

公告日期：2010 年 11 月 21 日

产地范围：四川省苍溪县境内所辖全部乡镇。

Changshou Shantian Pomelo was introduced to Changshou District, Chongqing City in 1887, with a cultivation history of more than 130 years. It originated from Shatian Town, Guangxi Zhuang Autonomous Region. Benefiting from the unique climate conditions as well as the purple soil and sandy soil planting environment at the Changshou Lake, the largest man-made lake in Southwest China and in the Basin of Longxi River, Changshou Shantian Pomelo has the unique quality of sweet pomelos. It looks like a bottle gourd, is thin-skinned and juicy, with yellow skin and plump flesh, contains rich nutriments, and is highly resistant to storage. It is hailed as "Natural Canned Food".

GI Profile

Notice Date: March 21, 2009

Producing Area: Dandu Town, Linfeng Town, Changshouhu Town, Yunji Town, Shuanglong Town, Longhe Town, Haitang Town, Shiyan Town, Gelan Town, Xinshi Town, Bake Town, Honghu Town, Wanshun Town, Fengcheng Subdistrict Office, Yanjia Subdistrict Office, Jiangnan Subdistrict Office, and Duzhou Subdistrict Office of Changshou District, Chongqing City.

长寿沙田柚

Changshou Shantian Pomelo

长寿沙田柚自1887年引入重庆市长寿区，栽培历史已逾130年，原产于广西壮族自治区沙田镇。受益于西南最大人工湖——长寿湖及龙溪河流域独特的气候条件及紫色土壤、沙粒土壤种植环境，长寿沙田柚形成了蜜味柚类的独特品质。其形似葫芦、皮薄汁多、皮黄肉厚、营养丰富、极耐贮藏，素有『天然罐头』之美誉。

地理标志概况

公告日期：2009年3月21日

产地范围：重庆市长寿区但渡镇、邻封镇、长寿湖镇、云集镇、双龙镇、龙河镇、海棠镇、石堰镇、葛兰镇、新市镇、八颗镇、洪湖镇、万顺镇、凤城街道办事处、晏家街道办事处、江南街道办事处、渡舟街道办事处。

The unique climate and soil of the old course basin of the Hutuo River in Jinzhou City, Hebei Province give birth to "Jinzhou Pear", which has a cultivation history of two thousand years. Jinzhou Pear has a smooth surface, thin peel, few stone cells, good color, more juice, sweet taste, and unique appearance. It is known for "being tender and crisp, and having no residue after chewing".

GI Profile

Notice Date: March 28, 2012

Producing Area: The administrative areas of 8 townships (towns) including the following specific areas: Dongzhuosu Town, Zhoujiazhuang Township, Donglizhuang Town, Zongshizhuang Town, Mayu Town, Yingli Town, Circular Economy Park, and Taoyuan Town in the southeast of Jinzhou City, Hebei Province.

晋州鸭梨

Jinzhou Pear

河北省晋州市滹沱河故道流域的独特气候和土壤孕育了晋州鸭梨，已有两千年栽培历史。晋州鸭梨具有果面光滑、皮薄、石细胞少，色佳、汁多、味香甜，外形独具特色的品质，素有『落地酥碎，嚼后无渣』之美誉。

地理标志概况

公告日期：2012 年 3 月 28 日

产地范围：河北省晋州市东南部。具体范围为：东卓宿镇、周家庄乡、东里庄镇、总十庄镇、马于镇、营里镇、循环经济园区、桃园镇 8 个乡镇现辖行政区域。

Fangxian Mushroom has bright color, attractive appearance, fragrance and smoothness, pure texture, and rich nutrition. It is rich in calcium, phosphorus, iron and other minerals and a variety of vitamins, which can enhance human immunity. Fangxian Mushroom, a wonderful gift given by the nature to human beings, not only is highly popular in China, but also is well received abroad, from ports and docks in the Southeast Asia, to the tables in France, Italy, Germany and other places.

GI Profile

Notice Date: July 1, 2008

Producing Area: 19 townships (towns) including Chengguan Town, Qingfeng Town, Damuchang Town, Mengusi Town, Jundian Town, Hualongyan Town, Tucheng Town, Hongta Township, Langkou Township, Shahe Township, Wanyuhe Township, Qiaoshang Township, Yaohuai Township, Shangkan Township, Jiudao Township, Zhongba Township, Baihe Township, Wutaishan Forestry General Farm, and Yaoping Township of Fangxian County, Hubei Province.

房县香菇

Fangxian Mushroom

房县香菇色泽好、外观美、清香滑腻、质地纯正、营养丰富，含有丰富的钙、磷、铁等矿物质和多种维生素，可增强人体免疫力。房县香菇是大自然给予人类的美好馈赠，不仅在国内深受欢迎，在东南亚港口码头以及法国、意大利、德国等地的餐桌上，也到处飘散着它的味道。

地理标志概况

公告日期：2008 年 7 月 1 日

产地范围：湖北省房县城关镇、青峰镇、大木厂镇、门古寺镇、军店镇、化龙堰镇、土城镇、红塔乡、榔口乡、沙河乡、万峪河乡、桥上乡、窑淮乡、上龛乡、九道乡、中坝乡、白鹤乡、五台山林业总场、姚坪乡 19 个乡镇。

Cangshan Garlic is also known as Rocambole. According to *Dongguan Hanji*, a history of later Han dynasty and internal palace record by many 1st and 2nd century authors, "Li Xun, a governor of Yanzhou , planted wheat and rocambole, and distributed them to his subordinates with nothing left". Cangshan Garlic has high edible value and medicinal value. It enjoys a high reputation both at home and abroad for its features such as large head and regular garlic clove, paper-thin skin, jade white color, sticky and spicy fragrance, rich nutrition, sterilization, detoxification, and elimination of dampness and distemper.

GI Profile

Notice Date: October 12, 2007

Producing Area: The administrative areas of 13 townships (towns) including Shenshan Town, Moshan Town, Bianzhuang Town, Yitang Town, Zhongcun Town, Jiazhuang Township, Sanhe Township, Nanqiao Town, Changcheng Town, Ermiao Township, Cengshan Town, Xingming Township, and Lanling Town of Cangshan County, Shandong Province (now known as Lanling County, Shandong Province).

苍山大蒜

Cangshan Garlic

苍山大蒜，亦称葫或葫蒜。据《东观汉记》载：『李恂，为兖州刺史，所种小麦、葫蒜，悉付从事，无所留』。苍山大蒜具有很高的食用价值和药用价值，其具有头大瓣齐、皮薄如纸、洁白似玉、粘辣清香、营养丰富、杀菌解毒、消湿祛瘟的特点，在国内外享有盛誉。

地理标志概况

公告日期：2007 年 10 月 12 日

产地范围：山东省苍山县（现山东省兰陵县）神山镇、磨山镇、卞庄镇、沂堂镇、仲村镇、贾庄乡、三合乡、南桥镇、长城镇、二庙乡、层山镇、兴明乡、兰陵镇 13 个乡镇现辖行政区域。

Fangxian Black Fungus has bright color, plump and big appearance, fragrance, smoothness, good elasticity, rich nutrition and unique flavor. Known as "Yan Er", "The King of Delicacies", fresh Fangxian Black Fungus "looks like a flying swallow", and more than 10 kg of black fungus can be obtained by soaking 1 kg of dried ones. As a natural blood-enriching food, it is also called the Human Scavenger.

GI Profile

Notice Date: November 3, 2008

Producing Area: 19 townships (towns) including Chengguan Town, Qingfeng Town, Damuchang Town, Mengusi Town, Jundian Town, Hualongyan Town, Tucheng Town, Hongta Township, Langkou Township, Shahe Township, Wanyuhe Township, Qiaoshang Township, Yaohuai Township, Shangkan Township, Jiudao Township, Zhongba Township, Baihe Township, Wutaishan Forestry General Farm, and Yaoping Township of Fangxian County, Hubei Province.

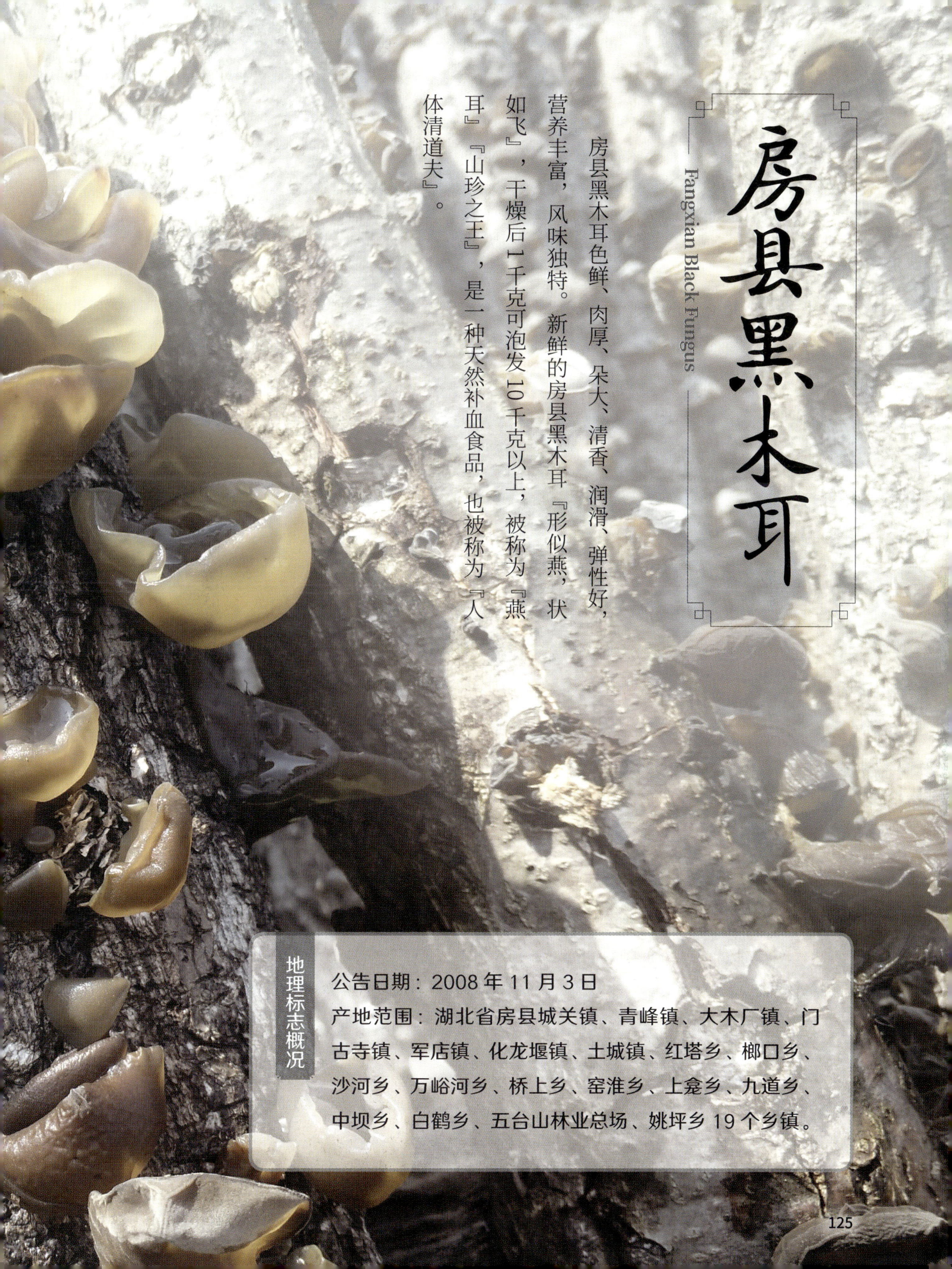

房县黑木耳

Fangxian Black Fungus

房县黑木耳色鲜、肉厚、朵大、清香、润滑、弹性好，营养丰富，风味独特。新鲜的房县黑木耳『形似燕，状如飞』，干燥后1千克可泡发10千克以上，被称为『燕耳』『山珍之王』，是一种天然补血食品，也被称为『人体清道夫』。

地理标志概况

公告日期：2008年11月3日

产地范围：湖北省房县城关镇、青峰镇、大木厂镇、门古寺镇、军店镇、化龙堰镇、土城镇、红塔乡、榔口乡、沙河乡、万峪河乡、桥上乡、窑淮乡、上龛乡、九道乡、中坝乡、白鹤乡、五台山林业总场、姚坪乡19个乡镇。

Pizhou City has a history of garlic planting for more than 2,000 years. With "green hills, clear water and fresh air", Pizhou's geographical environment gives Pizhou Garlic such characteristics as a large garlic head, white skin, crisp flesh, moderate spiciness, fewer garlic cloves, a neat shape, storage and transportation resistance, great commercial properties, rich nutrition and higher medicinal value. Pizhou Garlic, highly favored by domestic and foreign markets, has been regarded as top-grade garlic.

GI Profile

Notice Date: November 21, 2008

Producing Area: The administrative area of Pizhou City, Jiangsu Province.

邳州大蒜

Pizhou Garlic

邳州市有2000多年的大蒜种植历史，『好山、好水、好空气』的地理环境使邳州大蒜具有蒜头大、皮色白、肉质脆、辣味适中、蒜瓣少、形状整齐、耐储运、商品性佳、营养丰富、药用价值更高等特点。邳州大蒜被誉为大蒜中的上品，深受国内外市场青睐。

地理标志概况

公告日期：2008年11月21日

产地范围：江苏省邳州市现辖行政区域。

Xinghua Chive is a special vegetable variety bred in a unique natural geographical landscape which is known as "Duotian" (i.e., raised fields with irrigation canals) of Xinghua City and included in the "Globally Important Agricultural Heritage Systems (GIAHS)". With a moderate shape and a strong flavor, it has the health functions of increasing appetite and preventing cardiovascular diseases. It is an ideal raw material for freshness preservation and dehydration processing, as well as an indispensable condiment in healthy food. It sells well in more than 30 countries and regions in the international market.

GI Profile

Notice Date: December 22, 2006

Producing Area: The administrative area of Xinghua City, Jiangsu Province.

兴化香葱

Xinghua Chive

兴化香葱由『全球重要农业文化遗产』——兴化垛田这种独特自然地理环境孕育而出。其葱管适中，香味浓郁，具有增进食欲，预防心血管等疾病之功效，是保鲜、脱水加工的理想原料和健康食品中不可缺少的调味品。兴化香葱干制品在国际市场上畅销 30 多个国家和地区。

地理标志概况

公告日期：2006 年 12 月 22 日

产地范围：江苏省兴化市现辖行政区域。

Anqiu has a long history of ginger planting. After nearly 500 years of seed selection and cultivation, Anqiu Ginger features bright color, compact structure, large tuber and little fiber, and strong spicy flavor, with high edible value and medicinal value. Anqiu Ginger not only sells well in the European Union and Japan, but also becomes a supply product for the 2010 Guangzhou Asian Games, which proves its competitive strength again.

GI Profile

Notice Date: September 4, 2006

Producing Area: The administrative areas of 23 towns and subdistricts including Xing'an Subdistrict, Jiage Subdistrict, Linghe Town, Huangqibao Town, Zhaoge Town, Zheshan Town, Liujiayao Town, Guanwang Town, Dasheng Town, Wangjiazhuang Town, Huiqu Town, Baoquan Town, Jinzhongzi Town, Anshang Town, Linwu Town, Baifenzi Town, Shidui Town, Jingzhi Town, Shibuzi Town, Guanzhuang Town, Guangong Town, Hongshagou Town, and Wushan Town of Anqiu City, Shandong Province.

安丘大姜

Anqiu Ginger

安丘种植大姜历史悠久，历经近500年的选种培育，安丘大姜形成了色泽鲜艳、结构紧密、块大丝少、辛辣清香的特色，具有祛寒解表、止咳化痰、回阳通脉之功效，有较高的食用价值和药用价值。安丘大姜不仅畅销欧盟、日本，还成为2010年广州亚运会供应产品，再次证明了它的实力。

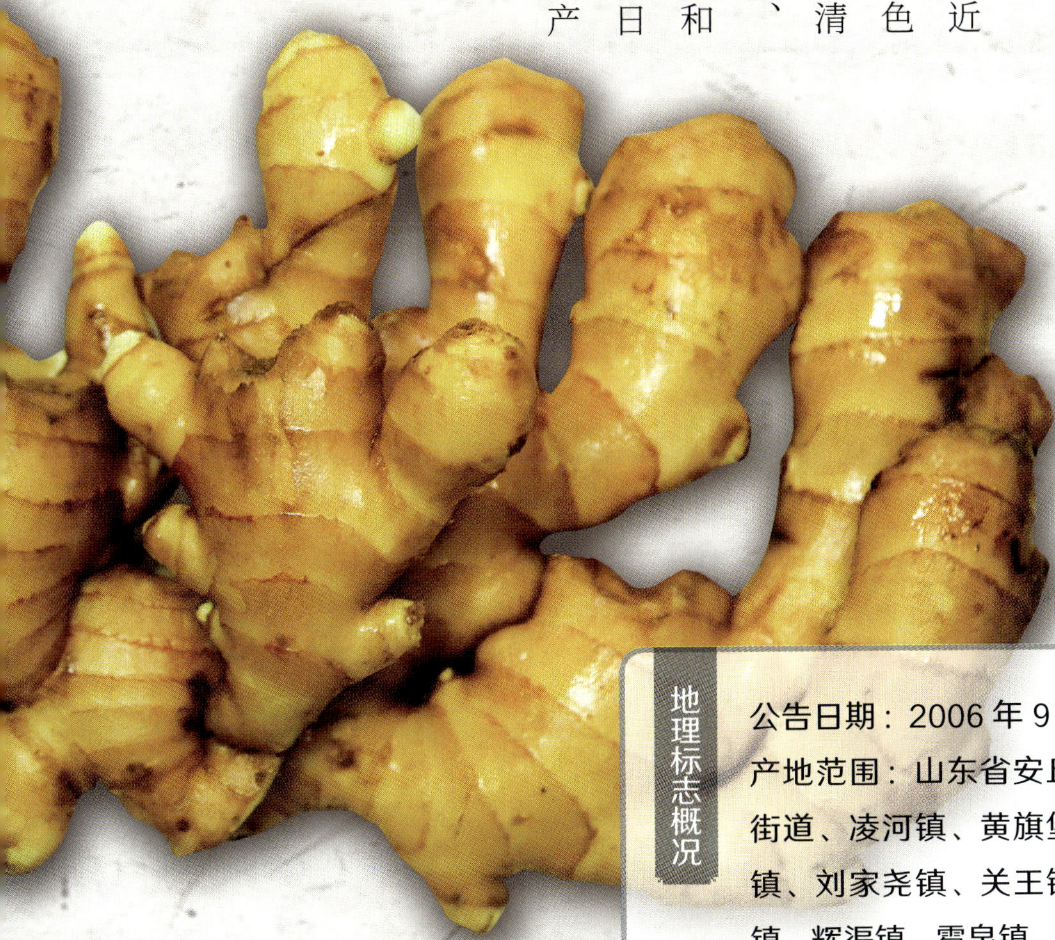

地理标志概况

公告日期：2006年9月4日

产地范围：山东省安丘市兴安街道、贾戈街道、凌河镇、黄旗堡镇、赵戈镇、柘山镇、刘家尧镇、关王镇、大盛镇、王家庄镇、辉渠镇、雹泉镇、金冢子镇、庵上镇、临浯镇、白芬子镇、石堆镇、景芝镇、石埠子镇、官庄镇、管公镇、红沙沟镇、吾山镇23个乡镇、街道现辖行政区域。

Jianning White Lotus Nut, commonly known as Jianlian, is produced in Jianning County, Fujian Province. Jianning is the "mother of Fujian region" and the source of Fujian water. The unique geological conditions have bred Jianlian of excellent quality. Its fruit is large in grain, round and regular, pure white, and easy to cook, without dispersing after being cooked for a long time. The cooked soup is clear in color, delicious and fragrant, glutinous and mildly sweet in taste. Jianlian planting began in 921 AD, with a history of more than a thousand years. It was an imperial tribute of successive dynasties.

GI Profile

Notice Date: July 21, 2001

Producing Area: The administrative area of Jianning County, Sanming City, Fujian Province.

建宁通心白莲

Jianning White Lotus Nut

建宁通心白莲俗称建莲，产自福建省建宁县。建宁是闽地之母，闽水之源，独特的地质条件孕育了优秀品质的建莲，其果实颗粒大、圆整，色如凝脂，粒大洁白，稍煮即熟，久煮不散，煮后汤色清，味香浓，入口粉糯清甜。建莲种植始于公元 921 年，已有一千多年种植历史，为历代皇家贡品。

地理标志概况

公告日期：2001 年 7 月 21 日

产地范围：福建省三明市建宁县所辖行政区域。

Luoping County, Yunnan Province, has been known as the "Hometown of Ginger" since ancient times. Its planting history can be traced back to the *Annals of Luoping County* in Qing Dynasty. Luoping Yellow Ginger is planted in areas at an altitude of 1,200-1,800 meters in Luoping County. Luoping County is warm and humid all year round, with sufficient sunlight and big temperature difference between day and night, which nurtures Luoping Yellow Ginger's unique qualities of fine texture, spicy taste, bright color, strong flavor, and eco-friendliness. It can refresh the brain and resuscitate the body after being smelled, and can invigorate the stomach and remove wind, cold and dampness after being eaten. Luoping Yellow Ginger can be called as top-grade ginger.

GI Profile

Notice Date: April 21, 2006

Producing Area: The administrative areas of Luoxiong Subdistrict, Lashan Subdistrict, Jiulong Subdistrict, Fule Town, Laochang Township, Changdi Township, Zhongshan Township, Jiuwuji Township, Banqiao Town, Dashuijing Township, and Lubuge Township of Luoping County, Yunnan Province.

罗平小黄姜

Luoping Yellow Ginger

云南省罗平县自古就有『姜之乡』之美誉，其种植姜的历史最早可追溯到清代《罗平州志》。罗平小黄姜种植于罗平县境内海拔1200—1800米的地区，长年温暖湿润、光照充足、昼夜温差大的气候条件铸就了罗平小黄姜质细纤小、味道辛辣、色泽鲜美、芳香浓郁、生态优质的独特品质，闻之可提神醒脑开窍，食之可健胃祛风寒湿邪，堪称姜中之极品。

地理标志概况

公告日期：2006 年 4 月 21 日

产地范围：云南省罗平县现辖的罗雄街道、腊山街道、九龙街道、富乐镇、老厂乡、长底乡、钟山乡、旧屋基乡、板桥镇、大水井乡、鲁布革乡。

Qingyuan Mushroom is hailed as "the champion of all kinds of fungi and the leader of vegetables" for its thick and round caps, short stalks, unique flavor, and rich nutrition. Qingyuan is the birthplace of artificial cultivation of mushrooms in the world. Dating back to the Southern Song Dynasty, a Zhejiang Qingyuan Mushroom cultural system, represented by mushroom cultivation, mushroom grower dramas, mushroom grower language, and mushroom kung fu, is formed through three major technological changes, which is an important heritage of Chinese agricultural culture.

GI Profile

Notice Date: January 9, 2002

Producing Area: The administrative areas of Qingyuan County, Longquan City, and Jingning She Autonomous County of Zhejiang Province.

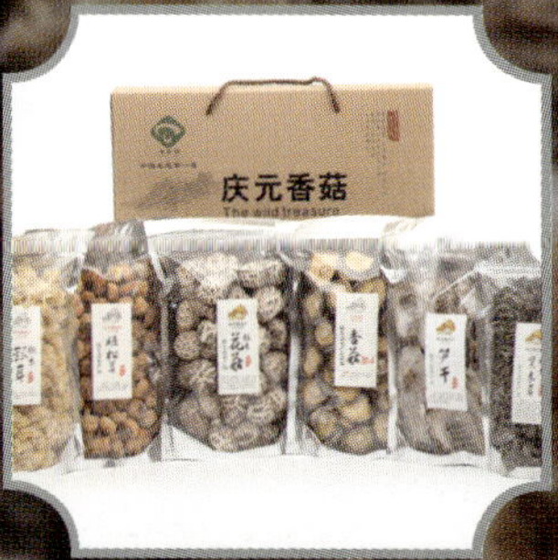

庆元香菇

Qingyuan Mushroom

庆元香菇菌盖厚且圆整，菌柄短，具有特殊香味，营养丰富，有『诸菌之冠，蔬菜之魁』之美誉。庆元是世界人工栽培香菇的发祥地，自南宋起，历经三次重大技术变革，形成了以香菇栽培、菇民戏、菇民语言和香菇功夫为代表的浙江庆元香菇文化系统，这是中国农业文化的重要遗产。

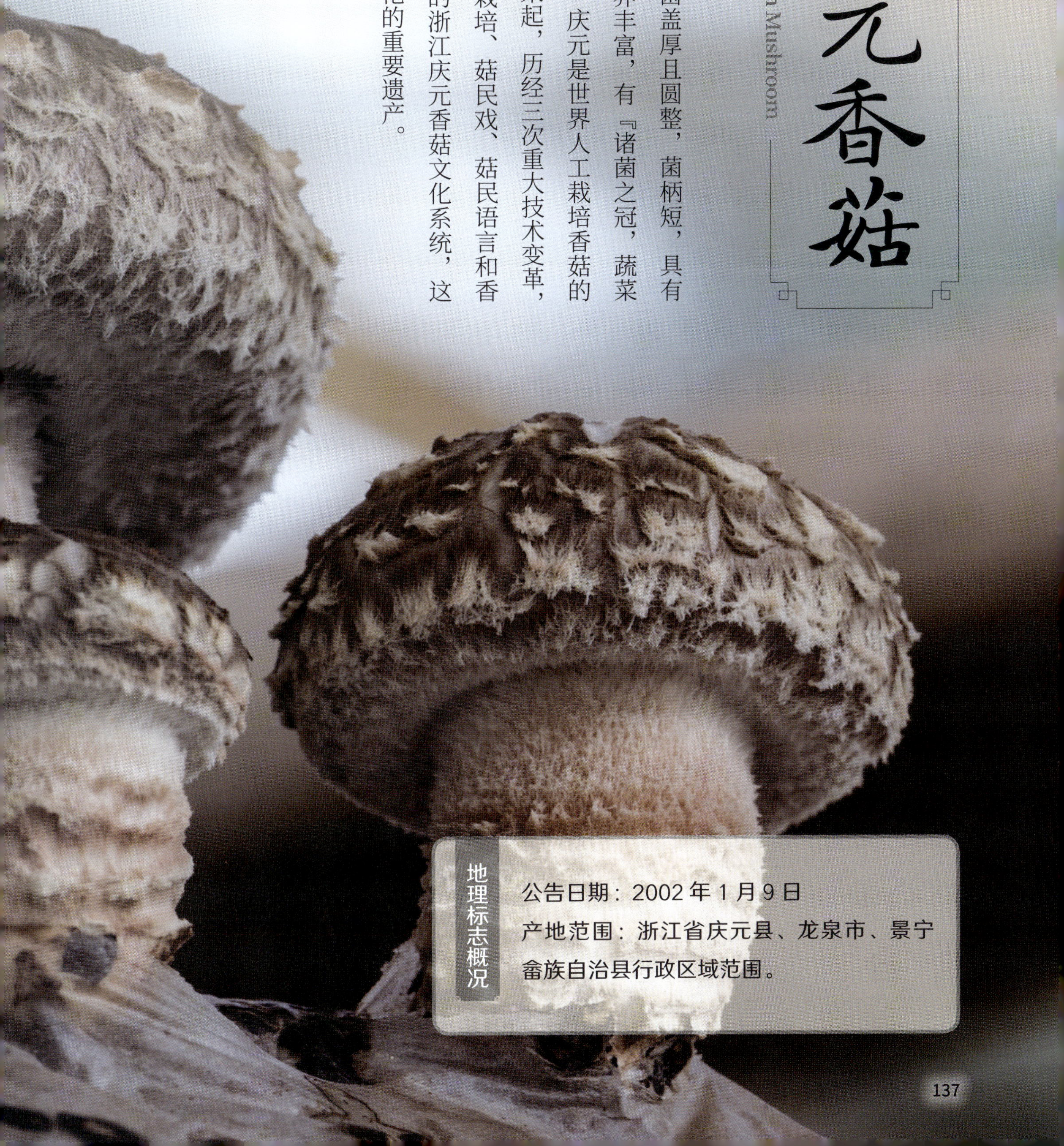

地理标志概况

公告日期：2002 年 1 月 9 日

产地范围：浙江省庆元县、龙泉市、景宁畲族自治县行政区域范围。

Located in the "golden line" for green mushroom production, Xixia County, Henan Province is a significant base for edible mushroom cultivation and production. Xixia Mushroom is good in quality, fully round in shape, natural in pattern, thick and delicious, aromatic in smell, smooth in taste, high in nutritional value. The products of Xixia Mushroom is of wide variety, encompassing six categories of raw mushrooms, canned food, leisure food, fermented sauces, food ingredients and seasonings, and functional health care food, which are favored by the market.

GI Profile

Notice Date : December 24, 2008

Producing Area: The administrative areas of 15 townships (towns) including Danshui Town, Tianguan Township, Yangcheng Township, Huiche Town, Wuliqiao Town, Dinghe Town, Chongyang Township, Xiping Town, Zhaigen Township, Sangping Town, Shijiehe Township, Miping Town, Junmahe Township, Shuanglong Town, and Erlangping Township of Xixia County, Henan Province.

西峡香菇

Xixia Mushroom

河南省西峡县地处绿色香菇生产的『黄金线』，是食用菌种植生产的重要基地。西峡香菇品质优良，朵形圆整，花纹自然，肉厚味美，气味芳香，口感爽滑，营养价值高，其产品丰富多样，分为原菇、罐头、休闲、发酵酱、食品配料调味料、功能保健六大类，深受市场的喜爱。

地理标志概况

公告日期：2008 年 12 月 24 日

产地范围：河南省西峡县丹水镇、田关乡、阳城乡、回车镇、五里桥镇、丁河镇、重阳乡、西坪镇、寨根乡、桑坪镇、石界河乡、米坪镇、军马河乡、双龙镇、二狼坪乡 15 个乡镇现辖行政区域。

The producing area of Hongyazi Peanut, higher in the northwest and lower in the southeast, is a hilly area that is a continuation of the Songling Mountains. Sandy loam peculiar to Hongyazi absorbs more heat during the day, and thus there is a large temperature difference between day and night, which is suitable for peanut planting. Hongyazi Peanut, produced in sandy soil of low mountainous and hilly areas in Hongyazi, has a low water content and no mildew, and an extremely low aflatoxin content, and is irrigated by using natural water and applied with farmyard manure, making the peanut a natural healthy food. It is bright in color, crispy but not hard, moist but not sticky, round and plump in kernel, uniform in size, and high in oil yield; and it contains rich vitamin E, calcium, zinc, iron, strontium and other trace elements essential to the human body.

GI Profile

Notice Date: September 3, 2010

Producing Area: The administrative areas of 7 townships (towns) including Hongyazi Township, Wanghai Township, Guojia Town, Weiping Township, Nanda Township, Shahousuo Town, and Jianchang Township of Xingcheng City, Liaoning Province.

红崖子花生

Hongyazi Peanut

红崖子花生产地地势西北高、东南低，为松岭山脉延续分布的丘陵地带。红崖子特有的沙壤土白天吸收热量多，昼夜温差大，适合花生的种植。红崖子花生产于红崖子低山丘陵区的沙质土壤，含水量低，无霉变，黄曲霉素含量极低，并使用天然水、农家肥灌溉，堪称天然健康食品。红崖子花生色泽鲜艳、口感脆而不硬，润而不黏，籽粒圆润饱满，大小均匀，出油率高；富含人体必需的维生素E及钙、锌、铁、锶等微量元素。

地理标志概况

公告日期：2010 年 9 月 3 日

产地范围：辽宁省兴城市红崖子乡、望海乡、郭家镇、围屏乡、南大乡、沙后所镇、碱厂乡 7 个乡镇现辖行政区域。

Jixian Apple grows in an altitude range of 820-1200 meters and borders the Yellow River to the west. The unique geographical location and natural environment have facilitated the excellent quality of Jixian Apple. Jixian Apple has the characteristics of regular and high-pile shape, smooth and delicate surface, bright and densely red color, crisp and sweet taste, high fruit density, and storage durability, etc. The fresh fruit has a sweet taste like syrup and an intoxicating aroma.

GI Profile

Producing Area: 8 rural towns including Jichang Town, Hukou Town, Tunli Town, Zhongduo Township, Checheng Township, Dongcheng Township, Wencheng Township, and Baishansi Township, and 79 administrative villages under the governance of Jixian County of Shanxi Province.

吉县苹果

Jixian Apple

吉县苹果生长在820—1200米的海拔范围内，该区域西濒黄河，独特的地理位置和自然环境，造就了吉县苹果的优良品质。吉县苹果具有果型端正高桩、果面光洁细腻、果色鲜艳浓红、口感香脆甜爽、果实密度大、耐贮藏等特点。鲜果甜味如饴，芳香醉人。

地理标志概况

产地范围：山西省吉县所辖的吉昌镇、壶口镇、屯里镇、中垛乡、车城乡、东城乡、文城乡、柏山寺乡共8个乡镇，79个行政村。

Zhalantun Black Fungus looks shiny in a dark brown color in the front and a light gray color at the back, naturally curled and uniform in size. A dried Zhalantun Black Fungus has a thick flesh and looks in a proper color; soaked in water, the Zhalantun Black Fungus shows its elasticity and rich luster, and has a delicate taste and a special flavor. Zhalantun Black Fungus is rich in phosphorus, carotene and a variety of micronutrients necessary for the health of human being, and contains far more vitamin B2 than ordinary grains and meat.

GI Profile

Producing Area: A total of 10 townships, towns (subdistricts), and 71 administrative villages thereunder, including Nanmu Elunchun Township of ethnic minorities, Halasu Subdistrict, Woniuhe Town, Samajie Ewenke Township of ethnic minorities, Moguqi Town, Guanmenshan Subdistrict, Sejilahu Subdistrict, Wadi Town, Haoraoshan Town, and Chaihe Subdistrict of Zhalantun City, Inner Mongolia Autonomous Region.

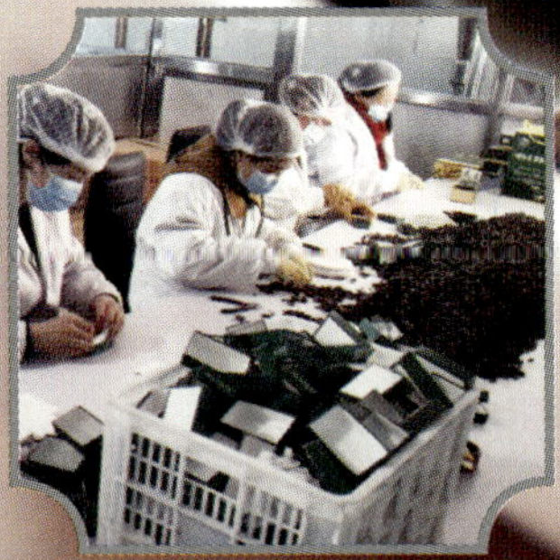

扎兰屯黑木耳

Zhalantun Black Fungus

扎兰屯黑木耳外观呈黑褐色，背面呈浅灰色，有光亮感，自然卷曲状，大小均匀一致。干时肉厚色正，泡开有弹性，富光泽，口感细嫩，风味特殊，含有丰富的磷、胡萝卜素和多种人体必需的微量元素，其中维生素 B2 含量远高于一般谷物及肉类产品。

地理标志概况

产地范围：内蒙古自治区扎兰屯市南木鄂伦春民族乡、哈拉苏办事处、卧牛河镇、萨马街鄂温克民族乡、蘑菇气镇、关门山办事处、色吉拉呼办事处、洼堤镇、浩饶山镇、柴河办事处 10 个乡、镇（办事处）及所属 71 个行政村。

The fruit bodies of Xiuyan Pholiota Nameko are mostly clustered, and the gills grow densely and straight. The cap is in the shape of hemisphere, dark brown or light yellow, with a smooth surface and egg white-like mucilage. Xiuyan Pholiota Nameko tastes crisp and refreshing, providing a unique flavor. It contains abundant essential nutrients for the human body, such as proteins, amino acids, iron, and calcium, and has a high content of crude proteins.

GI Profile

Producing Area: 24 rural towns of Xiuyan Manchu Autonomous County (Xiuyan County for short), Liaoning Province.

岫岩滑子蘑

Xiuyan Pholiota Nameko

岫岩滑子蘑子实体多丛生，菌褶密集直生。菌盖呈半圆形，深褐色或淡黄色，表面光滑，有蛋清状黏液。脆嫩爽口，风味独特，富含蛋白质、多种氨基酸、铁、钙等人体必需的营养成分，粗蛋白质含量高。

地理标志概况

产地范围：辽宁省岫岩满族自治县（简称岫岩县）境内的 24 个乡镇。

Dongning County, located in the southeast of Heilongjiang Province, is a major source of black fungus. Dongning Black Fungus looks in a pleasant color and tastes good with mushroom-like fragrance. The body of a Dongning Black Fungus is elastic, without roots, and looks in a dark brown color in the front and a dark gray color at the back, so it's easy to distinguish the front from the back and it's fair symmetry. It is also easy to reconstitute a dried Dongning Black Fungus, and the reconstituted Dongning Black Fungus has an oval outer contour, a beautiful appearance, a rich luster, and a complete shape without defects. Dongning Black Fungus is rich in iron, calcium, phosphorus and so on, especially having a high content of crude protein, crude fiber, and sugar.

GI Profile

Producing Area: The entire territory of Dongning County, Heilongjiang Province, from 130° 19′ 40″ to 131° 18′ 6″ east longitude and 43° 25′ 24″ to 44° 49′ 40″ north latitude, totaling 713,700 hectares.

东宁黑木耳

Dongning Black Fungus

东宁县位于黑龙江省东南部，盛产黑木耳。东宁黑木耳色泽好、口感佳，具有菌香味，耳片无根有弹性，耳面呈黑褐色，耳背呈暗灰色，反正面明显，对称度较好；易于复水，复水后耳片外轮廓呈椭圆形，外形美观、光泽度好、耳片完整、无损伤。东宁黑木耳富含钙、磷等，粗蛋白、粗纤维和糖含量较高。

地理标志概况

产地范围：黑龙江省东宁县全县境内，即东经130°19′40″至131°18′6″，北纬43°25′24″至44°49′40″，地域保护区面积713700公顷。

Le'an Bamboo Shoots have a complete body shape in a pyramid shape. Most Le'an Bamboo Shoots are hollow and uniform in size with natural color. The meat of the bamboo shoots is milky white or golden yellow with a fresh, tender, and refreshing taste. Having a naturally fragrant flavor, the Le'an Bamboo Shoots have a high edible rate. Le'an Bamboo Shoots are abundant in protein, total sugar, crude fiber, fat, and vitamin C content, and meanwhile, they are also rich in multivitamins, amino acids, carbohydrates and minerals, and the like.

GI Profile

Producing Area: 7 rural towns including Nancun Township, Gugang Township, Zhaoxie Town, Aoxi Town, Gongxi Town, Huxi Township, and Jinzhu Township in Le'an County, Fuzhou City, Jiangxi Province.

乐安竹笋

Le'an Bamboo Shoots

乐安竹笋笋体外形完整，呈金字塔状，多为空心，大小一致，色泽自然，笋肉呈乳白色或金黄色，口感鲜嫩爽口，具有自然清香滋味，可食率高。乐安竹笋的蛋白质、总糖、粗纤维、脂肪、维生素C含量丰富，同时富含多种维生素、氨基酸、碳水化合物及矿物质等。

地理标志概况

产地范围：江西省抚州市乐安县南村乡、谷岗乡、招携镇、敖溪镇、公溪镇、湖溪乡、金竹乡 7 个乡镇。

Tai Po Honey Pomelo has a large fruit and thin skin, the fruit is pear-shaped or obovate, and the skin is light yellow and smooth. The pulp is juicy and slag-free, moderately sweet and sour, with a fragrant honey flavor, and has few or no seeds. Tai Po Honey Pomelo has a high nutritional value and is rich in vitamin C.

GI Profile

Producing Area: Within the county area of Dabu County, Meizhou City, Guangdong Province, including 15 towns and farms such as Huliao, Baihou, Fenglang, Dadong, Guangde, Taoyuan, Gaobei, Dama, Sanhe, Zhourui, Yinjiang, Chayang, Xihe, Qingxi, and Fengxi Forest Farm.

大埔蜜柚

Tai Po Honey Pomelo

大埔蜜柚果大皮薄，果实呈梨形或倒卵形；果色表皮淡黄、光滑；果肉多汁化渣，酸甜适中，有香蜜味，种子少或无。大埔蜜柚营养价值高，富含维生素C。

地理标志概况

产地范围：广东省梅州市大埔县县域内，包括大埔县现辖下的湖寮、百侯、枫朗、大东、光德、桃源、高陂、大麻、三河、洲瑞、银江、茶阳、西河、青溪、丰溪林场15个镇场。

With a long history of mango cultivation, Baise City is in the dominant zone in the mid-ripening production of mangoes in China. The shape, color and quality of the fruit are all excellent. Baise Mango has orange-yellow pulp, less fiber, more juice, tender texture, and fragrant and sweet taste, with good resistance to storage and transportation, and high quality.

GI Profile

Producing Area: 58 townships and 712 administrative villages in 12 counties (districts), including Youjiang District, Tianyang County, Tiandong County, Pingguo County, Debao County, Jingxi County, Napo County, Lingyun County, Leye County, Tianlin County, Longlin County, and Xilin County, within the administrative area of Baise City, Guangxi Zhuang Autonomous Region.

百色芒果

Baise Mango

百色市芒果栽培历史悠久，是中国芒果中熟生产的优势带。百色芒果果形、果色、品质俱佳，其果肉橙黄，纤维少，汁多，肉质细腻，味道香甜，耐贮运，品质优良。

地理标志概况

产地范围：广西壮族自治区百色市行政区域内的右江区、田阳县、田东县、平果县、德保县、靖西县、那坡县、凌云县、乐业县、田林县、隆林县、西林县12个县（区）的58个乡镇，712个行政村。

Luoyuan *Pleurotus* Geesteranus is an artificially cultivated edible fungus, belonging to the pleurotus genus. It is a wild species found on the mushroom wood of Euphorbia royleana, and is very popular among consumers. Luoyuan *Pleurotus* Geesteranus has the characteristics of the fine white pileus, tender meat, and delicious taste of savory, mellow and sweet. It has high nutritional value.

GI Profile

Producing Area: 11 rural towns including Qibu Town, Songshan Town, Jianjiang Town, Fengshan Town, Feizhu Town, Zhongfang Town, Baita Township, Xilan Township, Hongyang Township, Huokou Township, and Bili Township in Luoyuan County, Fuzhou City, Fujian Province.

罗源秀珍菇

Luoyuan *Pleurotus* Geesteranus

罗源秀珍菇是人工栽培的食用菌，属于侧耳类，是在罗氏大戟的菇木上发现的野生种，深受消费者的青睐。罗源秀珍菇具有朵细质白，肉嫩味美，口感香醇、甘甜，食用可口的特点，具有很高的营养价值。

地理标志概况

产地范围：福建省福州市罗源县起步镇、松山镇、鉴江镇、凤山镇、飞竹镇、中房镇、白塔乡、西兰乡、洪洋乡、霍口乡、碧里乡 11 个乡镇。

Junan County has a long history of peanut planting. The natural conditions of light, heat, water, soil, etc. in this area are suitable for peanut growth. The produced Junan Peanuts are large and full with clearly netted pods, bright colored seeds, and various abundant nutrients, such as protein, vitamins, etc.

GI Profile

Producing Area: Within Junan County, Shandong Province, mainly involving 18 rural towns, such as Zhulu, Tuanlin, Pingshang, Wentuan, Laopo, Fangqian, Zhuanggang, Zhubian, Xiangdi, Xianggou, Banquan, Shilianzi, Tingshui, Dadian, Shizilu, etc. in Junan County, and a total of 723 administrative villages.

莒南花生

Junan Peanut

莒南县花生种植历史悠久，该地域光、热、水、土壤等自然条件较为适宜花生生长，所产的莒南花生个大粒饱，荚果网纹清晰，籽仁色泽鲜艳，富含多种营养物质，如蛋白质、维生素等。

地理标志概况

产地范围：山东省莒南县境内，主要涉及莒南县的朱芦、团林、坪上、文疃、涝坡、坊前、壮岗、洙边、相邸、相沟、板泉、石莲子、汀水、大店、十字路等 18 个乡镇，共计 723 个行政村。

Wendeng Apple is a kind of large fruit with a regular fruit shape. The fruit is mostly oblate, a few being nearly round. The peel is smooth and bright in color. The background color of the ripe fruit is light yellow, with dark red or bright red clouds or striped clouds covering above. The sarcocarp is yellow-white, dense, fine and crisp, and juicy. Wendeng Apple is with excellent sour and sweet taste, strong aroma, no astringency, and outstanding quality. The fruit is relatively durable in storage and transportation.

GI Profile

Producing Area: 15 towns (offices) within Wendeng City, Shandong Province, and 687 administrative villages in the development zone therein, starting from Dianzitou Village, Jieshi Town in the north to Gushi Village, Dashuipo Town in the east, Qiandao Village, Zeku Town in the south, and Xitanjiakou Village, Gejia Town in the west.

文登苹果

Wendeng Apple

文登苹果为大型果，果型端正，果实多为扁圆形，少数为近圆形。果皮光洁、色泽鲜艳。成熟果实果面底色淡黄，着暗红或鲜红色霞或条霞。果肉呈黄白色，肉质致密，细脆，果汁多，酸甜适口，芳香味浓，无涩感，品质极佳。耐储存和贮运。

地理标志概况

产地范围：山东省文登市境内的 15 个镇（办）、开发区的 687 个行政村，北起界石店子头村；东至大水泊孤石村；南至泽库前岛村；西至葛家镇西谭家口村。

Anqiu Chinese Onion is tight in pseudobulb, erect and long in welsh-onion stalk, and fine and crispy in nature. The tubular leaves are thick green, well-standing, heat and cold resistant, strong in disease resistance, fast in growth, early to be lunched into market, and high in content of trace elements such as selenium, zinc and iron.

GI Profile

Producing Area: 876 Natural Villages in Xin'an Substreet, Xing' an Substreet, Linghe Town, Jingzhi Town, Jinzhongzi Town, Huiqu Town, Shibuzi Town and Wushan Town under jurisdiction of Anqiu City, Shandong Province.

安丘大葱

Anqiu Chinese Onion

安丘大葱假茎紧实，葱白直立且长，肉质细脆；管叶为浓绿色，坚挺，耐热耐寒，抗病性强。安丘大葱生长速度快，上市早，产量高，硒、锌、铁等微量元素含量高。

地理标志概况

产地范围：山东省安丘市所辖新安街办、兴安街办、凌河镇、景芝镇、金冢子镇、辉渠镇、石埠子镇、吾山镇 8 个镇街道，共计 876 个自然村。

Xianghua Chilli has elegant figure, strong color, plumpness of nature, and strong spicy and fragrant tastes. The plants grow in tight clusters, the fruits are uniform in size, the young chilli is dark green, while the old chilli is bright red or purplish red; the chilli is plump, tender and crispy in nature, with a pleasant taste; it has strong spicy flavor; it's spicy and fragrant at the same time. Xianghua Chilli is rich in protein, fat, carbohydrates, calcium, phosphorus, potassium, etc.

GI Profile

Producing Area: Xianghua Town, Jiuchong Town, Houpo Town, Madeng Town and Cangfang Town of Xichuan County, Henan Province.

香花辣椒

Xianghua Chilli

香花辣椒形美、色鲜、肉厚、辣浓、味香。其植株生长紧簇，辣椒大小均匀，青椒呈深绿色，老熟椒呈红色或紫红色，光亮鲜艳；果肉厚，肉质嫩脆、口感舒雁；辛辣味强；辣香兼备。香花辣椒营养丰富，富含蛋白质、脂肪、碳水化合物、钙、磷、钾等多种营养物质。

地理标志概况

产地范围：河南省淅川县境内的香花、九重、厚坡、马蹬、仓房五镇。

Wuxi Potato has smooth skin, and is light yellow with gray and slightly shiny. The section is smooth and light yellow in color. After being cooked, it tastes crisp and soft, tender, and slightly glutinous, with faint fragrance.

GI Profile

Producing Area: All rural towns within the jurisdiction of Wuxi County, Chongqing City.

巫溪洋芋

Wuxi Potato

巫溪洋芋表皮光滑，淡黄带灰，略有光泽。切面平滑，色泽淡黄。蒸煮后口感酥软，细腻，微糯，淡香。

地理标志概况

产地范围：重庆市巫溪县辖区内全部乡镇。

Meixian Kiwifruit has a medium and uniform fruit size. The fruit shape is regular, pleasing to the eye, neat, and consistent; the fruit surface is clean; the sarcocarp is delicate, fragrant and juicy, sour and sweet, and refreshing with a mixed fragrance of various fruits; the fruit core is small; the sarcocarp is gorgeous and colorful, varying from green to red, yellow, etc.; it has many grains of seeds; it is shelf-stable and can stand long-distance travel; it has a long shelf life. Meixian Kiwifruit has a unique flavor and high nutritional value. The sarcocarp is abundant in sugar, protein, organic acids, vitamins, minerals, and 17 kinds of amino acids needed by the human body.

GI Profile

Producing Area: The western part of the Guanzhong Plain in the northern slope of Qinling Mountains and south of the Weihe River, in Baoji City, Shaanxi Province, stretching to Qinghua Village, Qinghua Township in the east, Yuguanying Village, Shoushan Town in the west, the shallow mountainous area of the northern slope of Qinling Mountains in the south, and Weihe River in the north, and involving 8 rural towns and 104 villages.

眉县猕猴桃

Meixian Kiwifruit

眉县猕猴桃大小适中均匀，果形端正美观，果面洁净，果肉细腻，浓香多汁，酸甜爽口，具有多种水果的混合香味；果心小；果肉艳丽多彩，有绿肉、红肉、黄肉等品种；种子粒多；耐贮耐运；货架期长。风味独特，营养价值高，果肉中含有丰富的糖、蛋白质、有机酸、维生素、矿物质和人体所需的17种氨基酸等。

地理标志概况

产地范围：陕西省宝鸡市秦岭北麓、渭河以南的关中平原西部，东至青化乡青化村，西至首善镇余官营村，南至秦岭北麓浅山区，北至渭河。涉及8个乡镇、104个村。

Liaozhong Rose has a long planting history in wide varieties. Liaozhong has a flat terrain and fertile soil, especially unique microclimate formed by the Liaohe River, with sufficient sunlight and humid air, creating dominant natural conditions for the growth of roses. The roses produced are dark and strong in flower color, beautiful in flower shape, strong and long-lasting in fragrance. They are regarded as top-grade roses.

GI Profile

Notice Date: August 14, 2012

Producing Area: The administrative area of Liaozhong County, Liaoning Province.

辽中玫瑰

Liaozhong Rose

辽中玫瑰种植历史悠久，品种繁多。辽中地势平坦，土质肥沃，特别是因辽河形成的独特小气候，光照充足，空气湿润，造就了玫瑰生长的优势自然条件。所产玫瑰花色深沉浓烈，花姿优美，香气浓郁持久，是玫瑰中的上品。

地理标志概况

公告日期：2012 年 8 月 14 日

产地范围：辽宁省辽中县现辖行政区域。

Ophiopogon japonicus is spindle-shaped with slightly pointed ends. With fine vertical lines and flexible texture, its surface is light yellow or grayish yellow. The cross section is yellowish white, translucent, and the central column is slim and short. It smells slightly fragrant and tastes sweet and a little bitter. It has the effects of nourishing Yin, promoting the secretion of body fluid, moistening lung and clearing away the heart-fire. Ophiopogon japonicus is a famous genuine Chinese herbal medicine and an important medicine for nourishing Yin in China. The cultivation of Fucheng *Ophiopogon japonicus* has a long history in Santai County. Since 1814, it had been widely planted in Luxi Town, Yongming Town and other places. It was mainly distributed in the middle reaches of the Fujiang River Basin. Its average annual output in Santai County is 15,000 tons, accounting for more than 70% of the total output in China and its export volume accounts for 80% of the country's total.

GI Profile

Notice Date: May 24, 2006

Producing Area: The administrative areas of 9 townships (towns) including Yongming Town, Huayuan Town, Luxi Town, Laoma Township, Liuying Town, Licheng Township, Zhengsheng Township, Lingxing Town, and Xinde Town of Santai County, Sichuan Province.

涪城麦冬

Fucheng Ophiopogon japonicus

麦冬呈纺锤形，两端略尖，表面呈淡黄色或灰黄色，有细纵纹。质柔韧，断面呈黄白色，半透明，中柱细小。气微香，味甘、微苦，具有养阴生津、润肺清心之功效，是我国著名的道地中药材和滋阴良药。三台县涪城麦冬种植历史悠久，早在 1814 年，已在芦溪镇、永明镇等地广为种植，主要分布于涪江流域中游地段。县内年均产量达 1.5 万吨，占全国麦冬总产量的 70% 以上，出口量占全国的 80%。

地理标志概况

公告日期：2006 年 5 月 24 日

产地范围：四川省三台县永明镇、花园镇、芦溪镇、老马乡、刘营镇、里程乡、争胜乡、灵兴镇、新德镇 9 个乡镇现辖行政区域。

Chaidamu Goji Berry is mainly produced in the Qaidam Basin, which has a unique plateau continental climate. The fresh fruit is exquisite and clear, brilliant red in color and large in grain, just like a ruby. The fruit is ovoid, has few seeds and thick pulp, and is uniform in size.

GI Profile

Producing Area: Within Haixi Prefecture, Qinghai Province.

柴达木枸杞

Chaidamu Goji Berry

柴达木枸杞主要出产于高原大陆性气候的柴达木盆地，鲜果玲珑剔透，红艳欲滴，状似红宝石，色红粒大，果实呈卵圆形，籽少、肉厚、大小均匀，味道甘甜，品质优良。

地理标志概况

产地范围：青海省海西州境内。

The fruits of Jinghe Goji Berry are berries which are large and plump. Fresh fruits are four-diamond or spindle-shaped, and dried fruits are bright red or purplish red. The fruits have thin skin and thick pulp, and a pure and sweet taste, without bitterness or astringency. There are no diseased berries, moldy berries, worm-eaten berries, broken dried berries, immature berries, or over-mature or mal-processed dried berries, and no impurities. The dried fruits are squeezed into a cluster, and scattered after being loosened.

GI Profile

Producing Area: Involving 56 central villages in 6 townships, towns and farms, including Tuoli Township, Daheyanzi Town, Bajiahu Farm, Aheqi Farm, Mangding Township, and Tuotuo Township of Jinghe County, Xinjiang Uygur Autonomous Region.

精河枸杞

Jinghe Goji Berry

精河枸杞果实粒大饱满，鲜果呈四菱形或纺锤形，枸杞果实为浆果，干果呈鲜红色或紫红色，果实皮薄肉厚，口感纯正、甘甜，无苦味、涩味，无病斑粒、霉变粒、虫蛀粒，无破碎粒、未成熟粒及油粒，无杂质，干果挤压成团，松开后呈散状。

地理标志概况

产地范围：新疆维吾尔自治区精河县托里乡、大河沿子镇、八家户农场、阿合奇农场、茫丁乡、托托乡 6 个乡镇场，涉及 56 个中心村。

The geographical environment and natural conditions of Otog Banner have created the unique quality of Otog Arbas Goat Meat. The meat has a tender texture, and is high in protein, low in fat, rich in amino acids and iron, and low in cholesterol. The meat has no gamey odor, and is delicious, juicy, refreshing in taste with a strong aroma.

GI Profile

Producing Area: The whole area of Otog Banner, with a protection area of 31.5 million mu in total, including 6 Sumu (a township-level administrative division in Inner Mongolia) towns including Wulan Town, Qipanjing Town, Mengxi Town, Mukainor Town, Arbas Sumu, and Sumitu Sumu, 75 Gacha (a village-level administrative division in Inner Mongolia) villages, 367 animal husbandry groups. The geographical coordinates range from 106° 41' to 108° 54' east longitude, 38° 18' to 40° 11' north latitude.

鄂托克阿尔巴斯山羊肉

Otog Arbas Goat Meat

鄂托克旗的地理环境和自然条件造就了鄂托克阿尔巴斯山羊肉的独特品质。其肉质细嫩，高蛋白、低脂肪，富含氨基酸和铁，胆固醇含量低，无膻味，味美多汁、鲜香爽口、香味浓郁。

地理标志概况

产地范围：内蒙古自治区鄂尔多斯市鄂托克旗全境，保护区总面积 3150 万亩，包括乌兰镇、棋盘井镇、蒙西镇、木凯淖尔镇、阿尔巴斯苏木和苏米图苏木 6 个苏木镇，75 个嘎查村，367 个牧业小组。地理坐标为东经 106° 41′ —108° 54′，北纬 38° 18′ —40° 11′。

Nanjing Salted Duck, as a traditional food, has a long history and prominent status. Nanjing Salted Ducks are made with exquisite craftsmanship. "Marinate the duck meat with fried salt, and soak the duck meat in clear brine" increase the mellowness of the duck; "dry the duck meat" reduces the duck fat to obtain thin and tight duck skin; "cook the duck meat enough with the cooking ingredients" maintains a tender and fragrant taste. The cooked salted duck has a plump body, fresh luster, white skin and tender meat, fat but not greasy, delicious and scrumptious.

GI Profile

Producing Area: The Administrative Division of Nanjing City, Jiangsu Province.

南京盐水鸭

Nanjing Salted Duck

南京盐水鸭作为一种传统食品，具有悠久的历史和突出的地位。南京盐水鸭制作考究，工艺精细。『炒盐腌，清卤复』，增加鸭的香醇；『炒得干』减少鸭脂肪，使其皮薄且收得紧；『煮得足』，使其食之有嫩香口感。做好的盐水鸭体型饱满，光泽新鲜，皮白肉嫩，肥而不腻，鲜美可口。

地理标志概况

产地范围：江苏省南京市行政区划范围。

Jinhua Pig has black skin and black hair at the head and rump, and white skin and white hair at the thorax, abdomen and limbs, and at the intersection of black and white, there is an obvious "halo" zone with black skin and white hair. The pig has thin skin and fine bones. The meat is bright red, has a tantalizing aroma, and tastes fat but not greasy.

GI Profile

Producing Area: 9 counties (cities, districts) including Wucheng District, Jindong District, Lanxi City, Dongyang City, Yiwu City, Yongkang City, Pujiang County, Wuyi County, and Pan'an County, and 151 rural towns (subdistricts) and 5,051 villages (neighborhood committees) of Jinhua City, Zhejiang Province.

金华两头乌猪

Jinhua Pig

金华两头乌猪头颈部和臀尾部为黑皮黑毛，胸腹和四肢均为白皮白毛，黑白相交处有明显的黑皮白毛的『晕』带。皮薄骨细，肉质鲜红，肉味香郁，肥而不腻。

地理标志概况

产地范围：浙江省金华市婺城区、金东区、兰溪市、东阳市、义乌市、永康市、浦江县、武义县、磐安县 9 个县（市、区）及市直、开发区所辖的 151 个乡镇（街道）、5051 个村庄（居委会）。

Tianzhu White Yak grazes in the alpine grassland, and the special climate and ecological conditions have created the unique quality of the beef. The fresh beef meat has glossy lean portions in uniform dark-red color and fat portions in orange color, and the meat is tight and springy with a natural beef flavor. The beef is high in protein and low in fat, and contains a variety of vitamins and minerals. The hair of Tianzhu White Yak has a high content of wool, and is pure white with excellent dyeability. Besides, the milk production of Tianzhu White Yak is high, and its milk is rich in nutrients.

GI Profile

Producing Area: 176 villages of 19 rural towns including Songshan Town, Xidatan Township, Huazangsi Town, Shimen Town, Zhaxixiulong Township, Dachaigou Town, Tiantang Town, Tanshanling Town, Haxi Town, Qilian Township, Danma Township, Maozang Township, Dahonggou Township, Dongdatan Township, Duoshi Township, Saishisi Town, Anyuan Town, Sailalong Township, and Dongping Township of Tianzhu Tibetan Autonomous County, Gansu Province.

天祝白牦牛

Tianzhu White Yak

天祝白牦牛放牧在高寒草原，特殊的气候生态条件造就了牛肉独特的品质。新鲜肉肌肉有光泽，深红色均匀，脂肪呈橘黄色，肉质紧密富有弹性，具有鲜牛肉的自然香味；牛肉高蛋白、低脂肪、富含维生素和矿物质。天祝白牦牛被毛含绒率高，被毛纯白，可染性强。天祝白牦牛产乳量高，营养丰富。

地理标志概况

产地范围：甘肃省天祝藏族自治县松山镇、西大滩乡、华藏寺镇、石门镇、抓喜秀龙乡、打柴沟镇、天堂镇、炭山岭镇、哈溪镇、祁连乡、旦马乡、毛藏乡、大红沟乡、东大滩乡、朵什乡、赛什斯镇、安远镇、赛拉隆乡、东坪乡 19 个乡镇的 176 个村。

Shengsi Mussels are produced in Shengsi County, Zhejiang Province, where abundant feed and excellent water quality provide unique natural conditions for the growth of the Shengsi Mussels. Shengsi Mussels are characterized by being big, full in meat, fresh, tender, and rich in nutrients, with a protein content level is high, and a moderate fat content. Shengsi Mussels contain eight kinds of essential amino acids that cannot be synthesized by the human body. Therefore, mussels have the reputation of "eggs in the sea".

GI Profile

Notice Date: June 8, 2012

Producing Area: The sea area within the administrative area of Shengsi County, Zhoushan City, Zhejiang Province, from 121 ° 30 ′ to 123 ° 25 ′ east longitude and from 30° 24′ to 31° 04′ north latitude.

嵊泗贻贝

Shengsi Mussel

嵊泗贻贝产于浙江省嵊泗县，丰富的饵料，优良的水质，为嵊泗贻贝的生长提供了得天独厚的自然条件。嵊泗贻贝具有个大、肉肥、鲜嫩、营养丰富等特点，其蛋白质含量高，脂肪含量适中，含有八种人体不能合成而又必需的氨基酸，有『海中鸡蛋』的美誉。

地理标志概况

公告日期：2012 年 6 月 8 日

产地范围：浙江省舟山市嵊泗县现辖行政区域内的海域，东经 121° 30′ 至 123° 25′，北纬 30° 24′ 至 31° 04′。

Donggang Surf Clam is very large, and its body is rounded triangle shaped. The clams at the shallow end are yellowish brown, while those at the deep end are dark brown. The shell has a smooth surface with growth lines which become more obvious towards the ventral margin, and also obvious at the anterior margin and the posterior margin, and the posterior margin is longer than the anterior margin. The umbo is purple, protruding from the dorsal margin and leaning toward the anterior margin. Donggang Surf Clam has thin shells and full meat, and its meat is tender and thick, and rich in protein, fat as well as various minerals.

GI Profile

Producing Area: The nearshore shallow water area of Donggang City, Liaoning Province. The east boundary is from 124 ° 08 ' 27.36 " east longitude, 39° 43' 31.51" north latitude to 124° 07' 39.54" east longitude, 39° 36' 40" north latitude; the south boundary is the 10 m depth contour; the west boundary is from 123° 30' 52.81" east longitude, 39° 45' 24.56" north latitude to 123° 31' 06.00" east longitude, 39 ° 38 ' 30 " north latitude; and the north boundary is the 0 m depth contour.

东港大黄蚬

Donggang Surf Clam

东港大黄蚬体型肥大，呈较圆的三角形，浅水区体色呈黄褐色，深水区呈黑褐色，壳表平滑，具生长纹，越近腹缘越明显，前后缘亦明显，后缘长于前缘。壳顶为紫色，突出背缘，偏向前缘。壳薄肉厚，肉质细嫩，肉体肥大，富含蛋白质、脂肪及多种矿物质。

地理标志概况

产地范围：辽宁省东港市境内近岸浅海水域。东界自东经124°08′27.36″，北纬39°43′31.51″至东经124°07′39.54″，北纬39°36′40″；南界为10米等深线；西界自东经123°30′52.81″，北纬39°45′24.56″至东经123°31′06.00″，北纬39°38′30″；北界为0米等深线。

Tongjiang Bass has a superior growth environment and a long history of breeding, with unique appearance characteristics of a long and slender shape and a flat cross-section; a silvery white ventral side; black spots mostly concentrated on the upper dorsal side, basically no spots below the lateral line; and light red mandibular muzzle, etc. The intrinsic quality of Tongjiang Bass is reflected in its high calorie, high protein and low fat, which has high nutritional value.

GI Profile

Producing Area: The Tongjiang River Watershed and the sea freshwater watershed within the Tongjiang River Estuary to Shacheng Port, between 27° 09′ -27° 22′ north latitude and 120 ° 11 ′ -120 ° 25 ′ east longitude, with a watershed length of more than 50 kilometers and a watershed area of 1,275 square kilometers.

桐江鲈鱼

Tongjiang Bass

桐江鲈鱼生长环境优越，养殖历史悠久，具有独特的外观特征：体形修长、横断面侧扁；腹侧银白色；黑色斑点大多集中于背侧上方、侧线下方基本无斑点；下颌吻端呈浅红色。桐江鲈鱼内在品质体现为高热量、高蛋白、低脂肪，具有很高的营养价值。

地理标志概况

产地范围：桐江溪流域和桐江溪入海口至沙埕港口以内的海淡水流域，介于北纬27°09′和27°22′之间、东经120°11′和120°25′之间，流域长度达50多公里，流域面积达1275平方公里。

The unique climatic conditions of Qianjiang area have developed the rich resources of aquatic plants in Qianjiang River, and sufficient natural baits, making it an ideal place for growth and reproduction of Qianjiang Crayfish and forging the excellent quality of Qianjiang Crayfish. A Qianjiang Crayfish has white gill filaments and a transparent abdomen, odorless, plump, clean. The two front chelicerae are thick and shiny. The shell of the body is generally light blue or light red. A mature individual is reddish brown with no attachments.

GI Profile

Producing Area: A total of 18 towns (subdistricts, districts) of Qianjiang City, Hubei Province, including Jiyukou Town, Gaoshibei Town, Wangchang Town, Guanghua Subdistrict, Zhouji Subdistrict, Yangshi Subdistrict, Zongkou Administrative District, Yuyang Town, Laoxin Town, Xiongkou Town, Longwan Town, Zhangjin Town, Haokou Town, Yunlianghu Administrative District, Xidayuan Administrative District, Yuanlin Subdistrict, Zhugentan Town, and Houhu Administrative District.

潜江龙虾

Qianjiang Crayfish

潜江独特的气候条件形成了潜江水草资源丰富、天然饵料充足的自然条件，是潜江龙虾生长繁殖的理想之地，孕育了潜江龙虾优良的品质。潜江龙虾腮丝洁白，无异味，外形肥大，腹部清洁透明。两只前螯粗大，色泽明亮，外壳一般呈淡青色或淡红色，性成熟个体呈红褐色，无附着物。

地理标志概况

产地范围：湖北省潜江市辖区内的积玉口镇、高石碑镇、王场镇、广华办事处、周矶办事处、杨市办事处、总口管理区、渔洋镇、老新镇、熊口镇、龙湾镇、张金镇、浩口镇、运粮湖管理区、西大垸管理区、园林办事处、竹根滩镇、后湖管理区 18 个镇（处、区）。

黄酒源于中国，是世界三大古酒之一。作为中国黄酒杰出代表的绍兴酒，因产于浙江省绍兴市而得名，贮存独特而芳香质佳，又称“绍兴老酒”。绍兴酒具有橙黄清亮、馥郁芬芳、甘鲜醇厚之风味，先后被列为中国“八大”“十八大”名酒之一，在1915年巴拿马万国博览会上获奖。

Yellow rice wine is originated in China and is one of the three ancient liquors in the world. As an outstanding representative of Chinese yellow rice wine, Shaoxing Rice Wine is named after its producing area of Shaoxing City, Zhejiang Province, and it has a unique storage method, fine aroma and high quality. Shaoxing Rice Wine is also called "Shaoxing Aged Wine". Shaoxing Rice Wine has a bright orange-yellow color, rich aroma, and sweet, fresh and mellow flavor. It has been listed as one of China's "Eight National Vintage Wines" and "Eighteen National Vintage Wines". It won a medal at the Panama Pacific International Exposition held in 1915.

GI Profile

Notice Date: January 31, 2000

Producing Area: (1) Special protection areas: from the Jishan Bridge in the suburb of Shaoxing City, Zhejiang Province in the east, to the west of main waters of Jianhu Lake between the Xikuahu Bridge in Hutang Street, Keqiao District, Shaoxing City, and the waters within 1,000 meters to the south and 500 meters to the north, and 1,000 meters upstream and 500 meters downstream of the waters of Xiguo Water Plant and Nanmen Water Plant. (2) General protection areas: the upstream waters of Jianhu Lake including Nanchi River, Potang River, Lougong River, Lizhu River, Qiuhu River, Xiangli River, Xingtang River, Xialv River and Xixiao River, and the downstream waters between the north side of the special protection area and Xiaoyong Railway of Zhejiang Province. Part of the land along the Jianhu Lake waters is included in the general protection area.

绍兴酒

Shaoxing Rice Wine

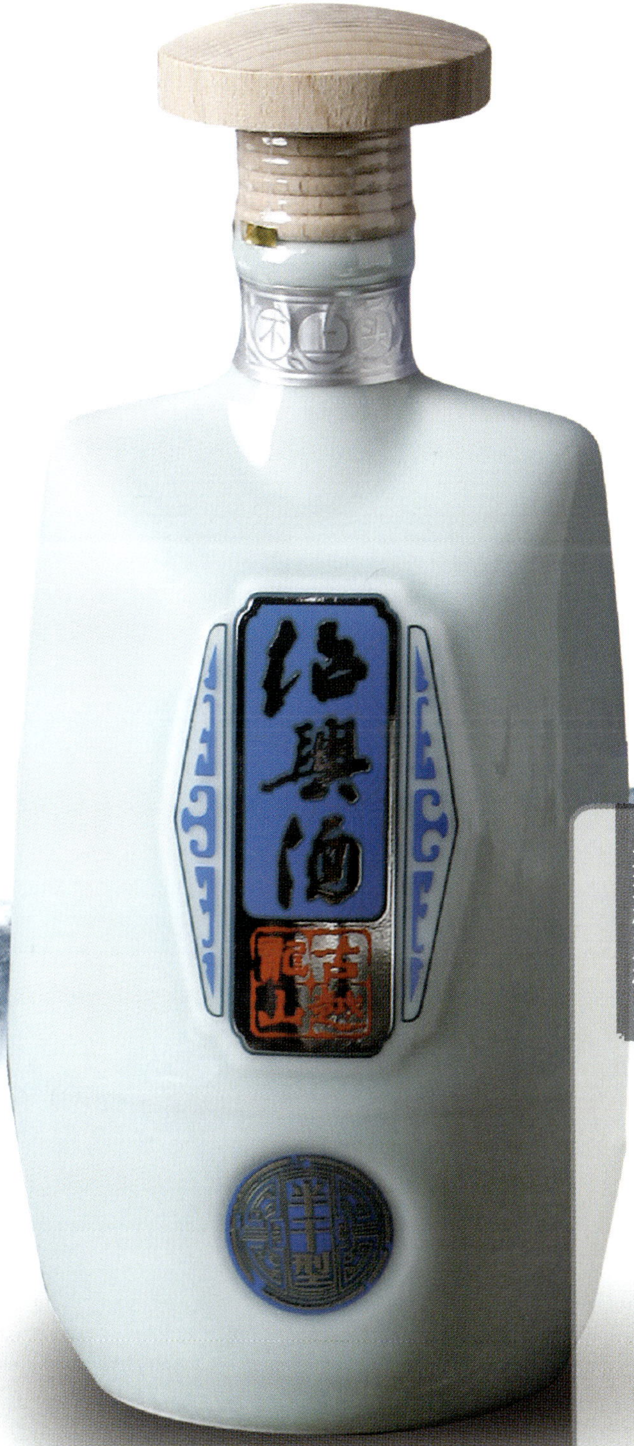

地理标志概况

公告日期：2000 年 1 月 31 日

产地范围：（1）特别保护区：东起浙江省绍兴市市郊稽山桥，西至绍兴市柯桥区湖塘街道西跨湖桥之间的鉴湖主体水域，及其南侧 1000 米、北侧 500 米内的水域，以及西郭水厂与南门水厂上游 1000 米、下游 500 米内的水域。（2）一般保护区：浙江省南池江、坡塘江、娄宫江、漓渚江、秋湖江、项里江、型塘江、夏履江、西小江等鉴湖上游水域，特别保护区北侧边界至萧甬铁路之间的下游水域。鉴湖水域沿岸的部分陆地列入一般保护区。

Huishui Black Glutinous Rice Wine is a precious rice wine produced by ethnic minorities (Buyi and Miao nationalities) in the mountainous areas of southwest China using high-quality black glutinous rice and natural mountain spring water over 1,200 meters as raw materials with the traditional process. The wine is black-red in liquor body, bright, transparent, and shiny without suspended matter; prominent in rice fragrance, elegant and delicate, lasting and obvious in fragrance, with the fragrance lingering on the emptied cup, and no foreign fragrance; and mellow, sweet, refreshing, coordinating, very exquisite and tender in taste.

GI Profile

Notice Date: August 23, 2012

Producing Area: The administrative areas of 25 townships (towns) including Heping Town, Gaozhen Town, Sandu Town, Baijin Town, Yashui Town, Duanshan Town, Lushan Town, Wangyou Town, Changtian Township, Doudi Township, Jialie Township, Gangdu Township, Ningwang Township, Yarong Township, Taiyang Township, Xiantang Township, Jiarong Township, Diji Township, Dalong Township, Daba Township, Baibang Township, Dima Township, Chang'an Township, Dayin Township, and Haohuahong Township of Huishui County, Guizhou Province.

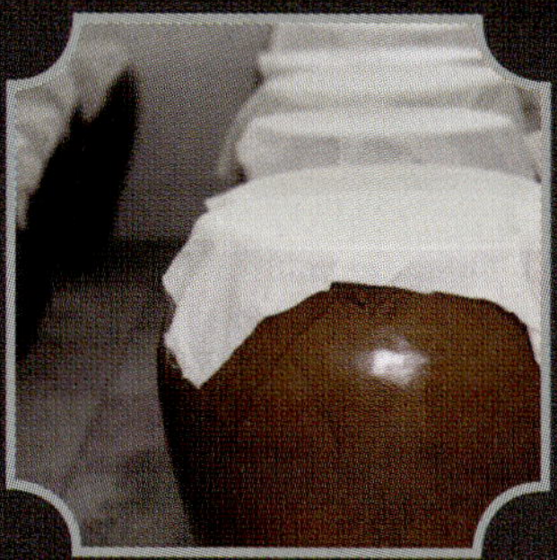

惠水黑糯米酒

Huishui Black Glutinous Rice Wine

惠水黑糯米酒是中国西南山区少数民族（布依族、苗族）以海拔 1200 米以上的优质黑糯米和天然山泉水为原料，并采用传统工艺制作生产的珍贵米酒。该酒酒体呈黑红色，晶亮透明、有光泽，无悬浮物；米香突出，幽雅细致，香味悠长明显，空杯留香，无异香；口感醇甜、爽口，协调，细腻感强，柔顺感强。

地理标志概况

公告日期：2012 年 8 月 23 日

产地范围：贵州省惠水县和平镇、高镇镇、三都镇、摆金镇、雅水镇、断杉镇、芦山镇、王佑镇、长田乡、斗底乡、甲烈乡、岗度乡、宁旺乡、鸭绒乡、太阳乡、羡塘乡、甲戎乡、抵季乡、大龙乡、大坝乡、摆榜乡、抵麻乡、长安乡、打引乡、好花红乡 25 个乡镇现辖行政区域。

The east region of Helan Mountain, which has sufficient sunshine, large temperature difference between day and night, little rainfall, and breathable soil, is one of the golden areas for growing wine grapes and producing high-end wines in the world. The perfect Yellow-River-based irrigation system guarantees the water and nutrient demand for grape growth. The produced wine is full and mellow accompanied by fruity aroma, emitting mineral aroma. The wine has a typical oriental style of "balanced sweet flavor and moisturizing effect" with unique characteristics.

GI Profile

Notice Date: January 30, 2011

Producing Area: The administrative areas of 30 townships (towns), farms, forest farms, and scientific research institutes including Chonggang Township, Xiamiao Township, and Qianjin Farm of Pingluo County; Jinshan Township and Nuanquan Farm of Helan County; Zhenbeibu Town, Xinjing Town, Nanliang Farm, Helan Mountain Farm, Agricultural Reclamation Scientific Research Institute, and Pingjibao Dairy Farm of Xixia District, Yinchuan City; Xingyuan Township of Jinfeng District, Yinchuan City; Wangyuan Town, Shengli Township, Zenggang Township, Lijun Town, Yinchuan Forest Farm, Huangyangtan Farm, and Yuquanying Farm of Yongning County; Ganchengzi Township, Lixin Town, Daba Town, Guangwu Township, Shuxin Forest Farm, and Lianhu Farm Branch of Qingtongxia City; Qukou Farm and Baima Township of Zhongning County; Hongsibao Town, Dahe Township, and Nanchuan Township of Hongsibao District, Wuzhong City, Ningxia Hui Autonomous Region.

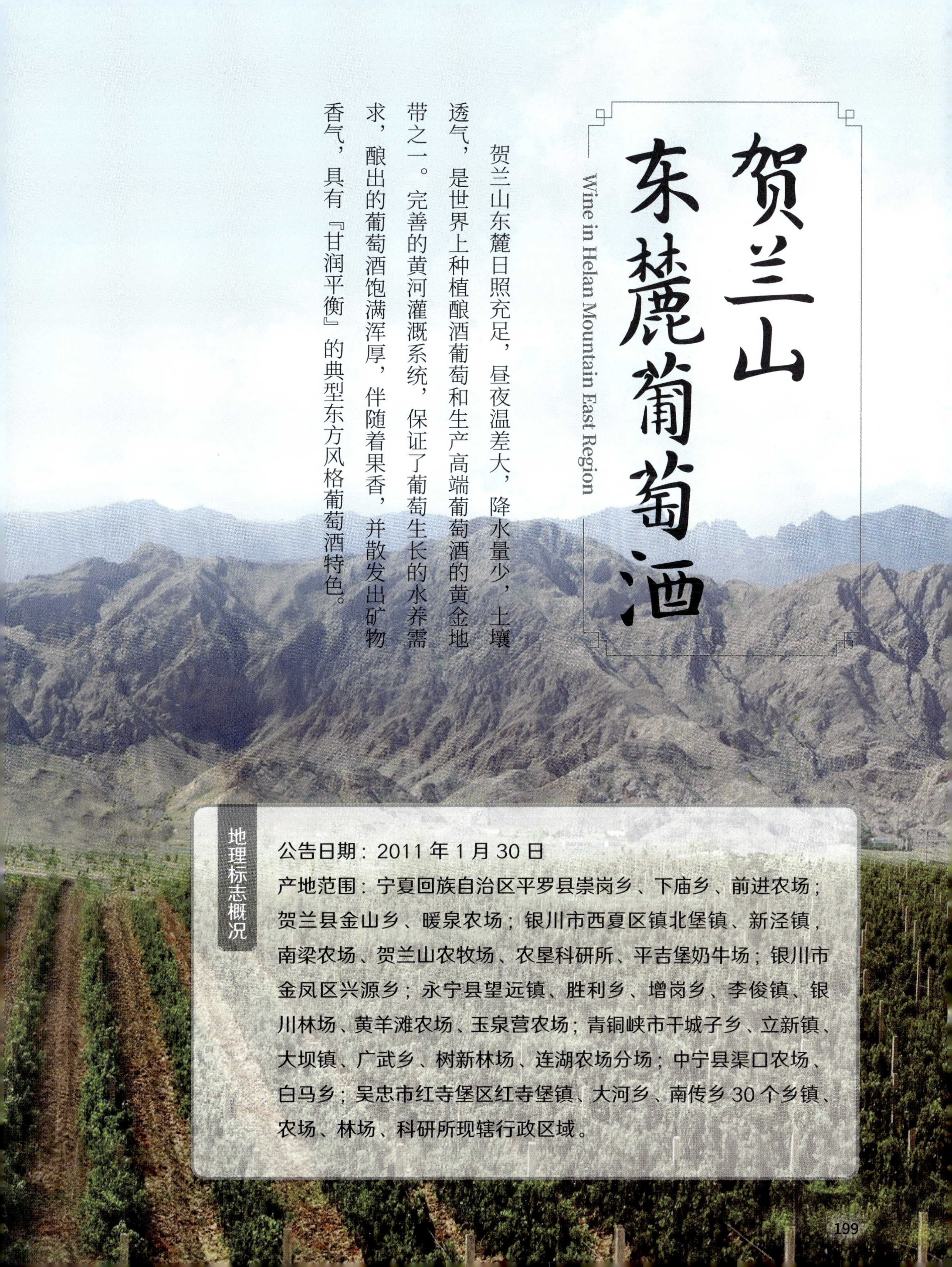

贺兰山东麓葡萄酒

Wine in Helan Mountain East Region

贺兰山东麓日照充足，昼夜温差大，降水量少，土壤透气，是世界上种植酿酒葡萄和生产高端葡萄酒的黄金地带之一。完善的黄河灌溉系统，保证了葡萄生长的水养需求，酿出的葡萄酒饱满浑厚，伴随着果香，并散发出矿物香气，具有『甘润平衡』的典型东方风格葡萄酒特色。

地理标志概况

公告日期：2011 年 1 月 30 日

产地范围：宁夏回族自治区平罗县崇岗乡、下庙乡、前进农场；贺兰县金山乡、暖泉农场；银川市西夏区镇北堡镇、新泾镇，南梁农场、贺兰山农牧场、农垦科研所、平吉堡奶牛场；银川市金凤区兴源乡；永宁县望远镇、胜利乡、增岗乡、李俊镇、银川林场、黄羊滩农场、玉泉营农场；青铜峡市干城子乡、立新镇、大坝镇、广武乡、树新林场、连湖农场分场；中宁县渠口农场、白马乡；吴忠市红寺堡区红寺堡镇、大河乡、南传乡 30 个乡镇、农场、林场、科研所现辖行政区域。

temperature below -8°C in the year in which the grapes have good maturity. Huanren Icewine is golden yellow in color with crystal clear appearance; it is rich in a variety of phenolic substances, accompanied by rich honey aroma and elegant floral and fruity aromas; and the sugar, acid, and alcohol content are harmoniously balanced, resulting in delicate and mellow taste.

GI Profile

Notice Date: December 31, 2006

Producing Area: The administrative area of Beidianzi Township, Huanren Manchu Autonomous County, Liaoning Province.

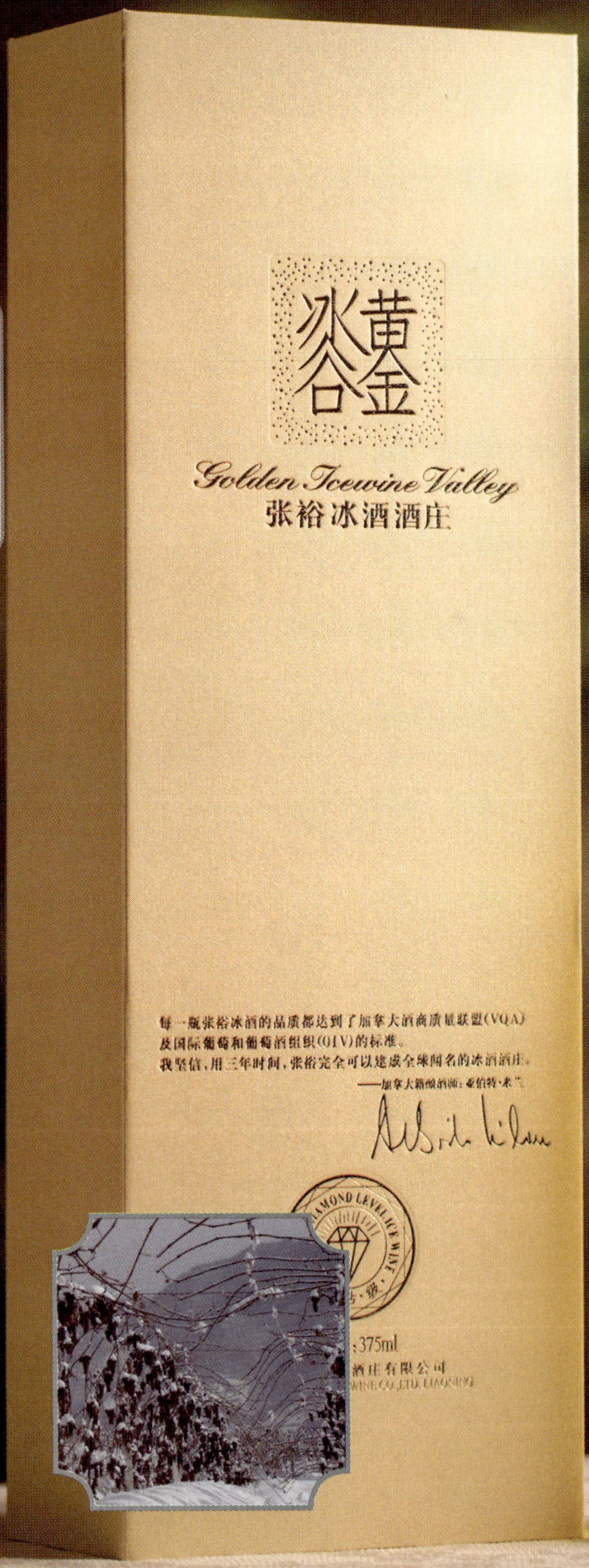

桓仁冰酒

Huanren Icewine

桓仁冰酒是一种甜型的静止葡萄酒，它是在葡萄成熟度好的年份，由在 -8℃以下采摘的冰葡萄压榨发酵而成的。桓仁冰酒色泽金黄，晶莹剔透；富含多种酚类物质，并伴有浓郁的蜂蜜香、优雅的花香、果香；糖、酸、酒度协调平衡，入口细腻圆润。

地理标志概况

公告日期：2006 年 12 月 31 日

产地范围：辽宁省桓仁满族自治县北甸子乡现辖行政区域。

Yantai City, Shandong Province is a major wine producing area in China. Yantai has an excellent natural environment for industrial development: a geographical environment with warm temperate zone continental monsoon climate, a terrain dominated by hills and low mountains, soil having high gravel content and good air permeability, and the "3S" elements required by wine: sunlight, sand and sea, making it the producing area that does not need soil bury in winter for cold prevention. The grapes planted under such conditions have balanced sweetness and sourness. Therefore, the produced wine is rich in fruity aroma, mellow and elegant, and balanced in structure, and possesses lasting aftertaste.

GI Profile

Notice Date: August 28, 2002

Producing Area: The administrative area of Yantai City, Shandong Province.

烟台葡萄酒

Yantai Wine

山东省烟台市是中国主要葡萄酒产区，具有优良的产业发展自然环境。该产区地理环境属暖温带大陆性季风气候，地形以丘陵低山为主，土壤砾石含量高、透气性好，拥有酿造葡萄酒所需要的阳光、沙砾、海洋『3S』要素，不需要冬季埋土防寒。在这种条件下种植的葡萄糖酸协调，酿出的葡萄酒果香浓郁、醇厚优雅、结构均衡、回味悠长。

地理标志概况

公告日期：2002 年 8 月 28 日

产地范围：山东省烟台市现辖行政区域。

The wine region of Shacheng Town, Huailai County (referred to as Huailai Shacheng hereinafter), located 100 kilometers northwest of Beijing (the capital of China) at 40 degrees north latitude, is a "golden zone" for grape growing. Surrounded by mountains, having the Sanggan River, Yang River, and Yongding River passing there through, the area has the features of four distinct seasons, sufficient sunlight, and a large temperature difference between day and night so that the unique climate is conducive to grape cultivation. This is the place where China's first dry white wine, China's first bottle of traditional sparkling wine, and China's first brandy that meets international standards were born. In 2001, Huailai County was named the "Hometown of Chinese Wine" by the Recommendation Committee of the Hometown for China's Specialties of the Ministry of Agriculture.

GI Profile

Notice Date: December 9, 2002

Producing Area: The administrative areas of 26 townships (towns) including Donghuayuan Town, Ruiyunguan Township, Xiaonanxinbao Township, Guanting Town, Sangyuan Town, Shacheng Town, Xibali Township, Dongbali Township, Dahuangzhuang Township, Xinbaoan Town, Cunrui Township, Tumu Township, Langshan Township, and Beixinbao Township of Huailai County in the Huaizhuo Basin at the confluence of Sanggan River and Yanghe River; Wujiagou Town, Zhangjiabao Town, Chengguan Town, Baodai Town, Luanzhuang Township, Huiyao Township, Heishansi Township, Fanshan Town, Wenquantun Township, Dongxiaozhuang Township, Wubao Town, and Wofosi Township of Zhuolu County, Hebei Province.

沙城葡萄酒

Shacheng Wine

怀来沙城葡萄酒产区地处首都北京西北 100 公里处，北纬 40 度葡萄种植的『黄金地带』，四周群山环抱，桑干河、洋河、永定河横贯其中，具有四季分明、光照充足、昼夜温差大等特点，独特的气候有利于葡萄种植。中国第一支干白葡萄酒，第一瓶传统法起泡酒，第一支符合国际标准的白兰地都诞生在这里。2001 年，怀来县被农业部中国特产之乡推荐委员会命名为『中国葡萄酒之乡』。

地理标志概况

公告日期：2002 年 12 月 9 日

产地范围：河北省桑干河、洋河交汇处的怀涿盆地内怀来县的东花园镇、瑞云观乡、小南辛堡乡、官厅镇、桑园镇、沙城镇、西八里乡、东八里乡、大黄庄乡、新保安镇、存瑞乡、土木乡、狼山乡、北辛堡乡；涿鹿县的武家沟镇、张家堡镇、城关镇、保岱镇、栾庄乡、辉耀乡、黑山寺乡、矾山镇、温泉屯乡、东小庄乡、五堡镇、卧佛寺乡 26 个乡镇现辖行政区域。

剑南春酒甄选优质高粱、大米、糯米、小麦、玉米五种粮食为原料，采用传承千年的古老秘法酿造技艺，经古窖池发酵，经年贮存，精心勾调而成。其酒体具有芳香浓郁、纯正典雅、醇厚绵柔、甘洌净爽、余香悠长、香味谐调、丰满圆润的典型独特的风格特征。

李肇的《唐国史补》对天下名酒记载道："酒则有……乌程之若下……剑南之烧春……"，并将剑南春酒作为宫廷御酒载于《后唐书·德宗本纪》。

Jian Nan Chun Liquor is prepared by selecting five kinds of high-quality grains of sorghum, rice, glutinous rice, wheat, and corn as raw materials, and adopting the ancient secret method that has been passed down for a millennium as the brewing technique through fermentation in ancient cellars, long-term storage and elaborate blending. The liquor body has peculiar characteristics of being rich in aroma, pure and elegant, thick and soft, sweet and clean, lasting in aftertaste, harmonious in fragrance, and full and mellow.

Li Zhao wrote about vintage wines all over China in *Supplement to the National History of Tang Dynasty*: "Concerning liquors...there are Wu Cheng Ruo Xia liquor... Jian Nan Shao Chun liquor...". Jian Nan Chun Liquor is also recorded in *The Book of Emperor Dezong about Later Tang Dynasty* as a royal liquor for the imperial court.

GI Profile

Notice Date: May 9, 2005

Producing Area: The administrative area of Jiannan Town, Mianzhu City, Sichuan Province.

剑南春酒

Jian Nan Chun Liquor

地理标志概况

公告日期：2005年5月9日

产地范围：四川省绵竹市剑南镇现辖行政区域。

古诗有云：“汉三杰闻香下马，高炉酒十里飘香”。高炉家酒（高炉酒）产自安徽省涡阳县高炉镇，当地独特的自然环境和深厚的道家文化底蕴造就了高炉家酒的独特品质。在浓香型白酒传统酿造技艺的基础上，高炉家酒采用双轮发酵、双轮窖藏的特色酿造工艺制成，酒体色泽清亮透明，口感绵甜净爽，回味悠长。

There is a saying in an ancient poem: "Three political celebrities of the Han Dynasty dismount from their horses after smelling the wine fragrance, as the fragrance of the Gao Lu Liquor is wafted far away". Gao Lu Jia Liquor (Gao Lu Liquor) is produced in Gaolu Town, Guoyang County, Anhui Province. The unique local natural environment and profound Taoist cultural deposits have created the unique quality of Gao Lu Jia Liquor. Gao Lu Jia Liquor is prepared by adopting the distinctive brewing process of double-round fermentation and double-round cellaring on the basis of the traditional brewing technique of strong aromatic Chinese spirits. The liquor body has a clear and transparent color, and a soft, sweet, clean and fresh taste.

GI Profile

Notice Date: December 23, 2013

Producing Area: The administrative area of Gaolu Town, Guoyang County, Anhui Province.

高炉家酒（高炉酒）

Gao Lu Jia Liquor/ Gao Lu Liquor

地理标志概况

公告日期：2013 年 12 月 23 日

产地范围：安徽省涡阳县高炉镇现辖行政区域。

扳倒井酒原产于山东省高青县，位于北纬 37 度世界黄金名酒带，地处万里黄河最后一道弯“安澜湾”生态湿地。扳倒井酒秉承多轮次优质糟醅“阳阴发酵”“井窖工艺”等酿酒要术，采用当地生产的优质春高粱、春大米、春玉米、冬小麦、黄河小米、黄河糯米等多粮配料，经高温堆积，大麸结合，多微共酵，陈年贮存，五型勾调，自成一格。

Ban Dao Jing Liquor is originally produced in Gaoqing County, Shandong Province, which is located in the world's vintage wine belt at 37 degrees north latitude and the ecological wetland of "Anlan Bay" , the last bend of the Yellow River. Ban Dao Jing Liquor adheres to key winemaking techniques such as many rounds of high-quality fermented grains undergoing "Yin-Yang fermentation" (double fermentations) and "well-pit process". Ban Dao Jing Liquor is prepared by using locally produced high-quality spring sorghum, spring rice, spring corn, winter wheat, Yellow River millet, Yellow River glutinous rice and other multiple grain ingredients. Then the ingredients are piled at high temperature, and combined with big bran; co-fermentation is carried out on multiple microbes; years of storage and five-type blending technology are adopted, forming a unique style.

GI Profile

Notice Date: September 30, 2010

Producing Area: The administrative area of Gaoqing County, Shandong Province.

扳倒井酒

Ban Dao Jing Liquor

地理标志概况

公告日期：2010 年 9 月 30 日

产地范围：山东省高青县现辖行政区域。

五粮液于 1909 年正式得名。产区宜宾为酿造五粮液提供了得天独厚、不可复制的生态环境。五粮液以高粱、大米、糯米、小麦、玉米为原料，利用“包包曲”为发酵动力，川南独有黄黏土为窖泥，采用分层入窖、分层起糟、分层蒸馏、跑窖循环、量质摘酒、按质并坛、分级储存的传统技艺，配以勾调技术调制而成。成品五粮液“香气悠久，味醇厚，入口甘美，入喉净爽，各味谐调，恰到好处”，尤以酒味全面而著称。

Wuliangye Liquor gained its present name in 1909. Yibin, the producing area, provides a unique and non-replicable ecological environment for brewing the Wuliangye Liquor. The liquor is made by using sorghum, rice, glutinous rice, wheat, and corn as raw materials, the "Baobaoqu" (wrapped starter) as the fermentation power, and the exclusive yellow clay in southern Sichuan as the cellar mud. With the traditional process of layered placement into the cellar, layered taking of distilled grains, layered distillation, cellar cycling, liquor storage according to quality, quality-based altar combination, and grading storage, Wuliangye Liquor is prepared with blending techniques. The finished product of Wuliangye Liquor has "lasting fragrance, mellow taste, luscious flavor, throat refreshing, and just right taste with mixed flavors", especially being well-known for the comprehensive liquor flavors.

GI Profile

Notice Date: November 30, 2001

Producing Area: The administrative areas can be divided into three parts: the Jiangbei production area is located in the north of Yibin City, Sichuan Province, and the "Wuliangye Industrial Park" on the shore of the Minjiang River covers an area of about 10 square kilometers; the production area of the old city is located in Gulou Street, Changchun Street, North Street, Donghao Street, Xianfu Street, Shunhe Street at the confluence of the Minjiang River, the Yangtze River and the Jinsha River, covering an area of more than 6,800 square meters; the South Bank production area is located on the south bank of the Jinsha River, covering an area of more than 50,000 square meters.

五粮液

Wuliangye Liquor

地理标志概况

公告日期：2001 年 11 月 30 日

产地范围：分为三个部分：江北生产区域位于四川省宜宾市北面，岷江之滨的“五粮液工业园区”，占地约 10 平方公里；老城区生产区域分布在岷江、长江、金沙江三江汇合处的鼓楼街、长春街、北街、东浩街、县府街、顺河街，占地 6800 多平方米；南岸生产区域位于金沙江的南岸，占地 5 万多平方米。

Moutai Liquor is one of the three major distilled liquors in the world and enjoys a high reputation both at home and abroad. It is produced in Maotai Town, Guizhou Province. With the unique natural environment, Moutai Liquor is elaborately brewed by using local high-quality glutinous sorghum, wheat, and water as raw materials through scientific and distinctive traditional technique over five years. The liquor has the characteristics of outstanding sauce flavor fragrance, elegancy and delicacy, mellow liquor body, lasting aftertaste, and lasting fragrance left in an emptied cup.

GI Profile

Notice Date: March 29, 2001

Producing Area: Maotai Town, Renhuai City, Guizhou Province, from the Xiaohe Power Station at the outlet of Yanjin River of Maotai Town in the south, ending at Yangliu Bay of the workshop 1 of Maotai Distillery in the north, and the section from Yangchajie Road of Yangliu Bay to Maozun Highway as the northern boundary, the section from Maozun Highway to Red Brick Factory to the southern of Yanjin River as the eastern boundary, west to Chishui River and Chishui River as western boundary, which is about 7.5 square kilometers. Extending from this area to the south, located in the canyon zone of Chishui River, east by Zhidong Mountain and the main peak of Mafuxi, connected with Chishui River in the west, connected Taiping Village in the south and ends at the boundary of Yantang Valley, connected with the Xiaohekou of Yanjin River in the north and connected with the original area, the extension area is about 7.53 square kilometers, and the total area is about 15.03 square kilometers.

茅台酒（贵州茅台酒）

Moutai Liquor / Kweichow Moutai Liquor

茅台酒是世界三大蒸馏酒之一，在国内外享有盛名。茅台酒产于贵州省茅台镇，以本地优质糯高粱、小麦、水为原料，利用得天独厚的自然环境，采用科学独特的传统工艺精心酿制，历经五年而成。具有酱香突出、幽雅细腻、酒体醇厚、回味悠长、空杯留香持久的特点。

地理标志概况

公告日期：2001 年 3 月 29 日

产地范围：贵州省仁怀市茅台镇内，南起茅台镇地辖的盐津河出水口的小河电站，北止于茅台酒厂一车间的杨柳湾，并以杨柳湾羊叉街路上到茅遵公路段为北界，东以茅遵公路至红砖厂到盐津河南端地段为界，西至赤水河，以赤水河为界，约 7.5 平方公里。从该范围往南延伸，地处赤水河峡谷地带，东靠智动山、马福溪主峰，西接赤水河，南接太平村以堰塘沟界止，北接盐津河小河口与原范围相接，延伸面积约 7.53 平方公里，总面积共约 15.03 平方公里。

查找相关信息

在线

国家知识产权局官网

https://www.cnipa.gov.cn

地理标志

https://www.cnipa.gov.cn/col/col1388/index.html